Fruit of the Spirit

Written by Darold Edwards

Fruit of the Spirit

Table of Contents:

i. A General Introduction to
The Works of

Darold Edwards

I would like to begin this introduction of myself and my writings with a greeting to all who are gracious enough to take the time to read my writings and join me in this journey of Bible exploration and study. This greeting is found in **[2 Peter 1: 2], "Grace and peace be multiplied to you through the knowledge of God, and of Jesus our Lord".** In **[Galatians 2: 6] Paul writes of people "who added nothing to me".** It is my desire and prayer that these writings will add much to you in your Bible explorations and enrichment of life.

Let me introduce myself to you. It is very likely you have never heard of me but that is alright, as I have never heard of the vast majority of you, but, I know you are out there somewhere in our big wide world that seems to be getting smaller with a disturbing amount of consistency. At the present time I am 75 years old, and like most of everything else in this world, my age is subject to constant change. My wife of 52, going on 53years of marriage, Patricia, is a very wonderful person who has had the grace to put up with me these many years gone by and has been a constant source of help, strength, and encouragement to me; with a little challenge thrown in from time to time to help keep life interesting. But having no complaints, I am looking forward to a continuation of our life together, at least for some time to come. We have our home in Albany, Oregon, raised 3 children there and have grandchildren and great grandchildren.

After a privileged time as a child and young person under the care and guidance of some very wonderful loving parents, I proceeded on to adulthood with an average course of life doing some things I should and some that I shouldn't. My specific vocation, after various jobs, was about 42 years as an electrician which was enjoyed very much. In the latter portion of this time I was able and blessed to assist in many church construction jobs as an electrician. There came a time, however, that my body convinced me it was time to seek other easier things to do. After that career ran its course and was fading into the sunset, I was led into an interest in writing, which is where I am today and will probably be for the remainder of my time on this earth. I am enjoying it with much satisfaction, and what you see here is among the beginnings of it. I hope you will blessed by it.

My main interest and priority is and has been in pursuit of Biblical study and knowledge for several years. As I get an ever increasing **"Vision of the Value"** of such study and exploration, the interest and priority increases accordingly. This Biblical knowledge with its provision of life and life more abundantly through Jesus Christ our Lord, indeed has become my life with its great and perfect peace with joy unspeakable and full of glory. What a blessed state of being to enjoy an unending hope and blessed assurance of a future that extends from today on to and including eternity.

Not being very impressed with humanity in its general condition and what it has done to this world God has provided for it, much of my writings will be addressing this issue and whose responsible for such a degraded condition as this world is in, including our "Land of the Free and the Home of the Brave". You may not agree with me in some of my views and interpretations, but it is only important that you be in agreement with Jesus. Some of the positions I take on traditional Bible interpretations will be somewhat controversial, maybe even viewed as heretical by some, but will certainly provide reason for some new exploration of thinking and thought. God tells us in **[Isaiah 55: 8-9], "My thoughts are not your thoughts, neither are my ways your ways, saith the Lord. For as the**

heavens are higher than the earth, so are my ways higher than your ways, and my thoughts than your thoughts".

So as we re-explore some of these old traditional truths and absolutes of God's Word that have brought life, strength, stability, and comfort to all who embrace them, lets keep our minds open to other additional concepts, original ideas, thoughts and ways that are a part of the expanse between where we are today and where God is calling us to be. I do not believe, that in the fullness of God's greatness, man has reached the end of all God has for us to think about either in the knowledge we are to gain or in the development of our mental capabilities. Much education and knowledge lay before us yet to be attained to. Once again, it is not important that you agree with me, but don't get caught in disagreement with God and his Word, that is a fatal mistake that is much to prevalent in our world today.

My writings are not meant to be entertaining, though a bit of mirth from time to time is acceptable. Yet encouragement and inspiration for meditation and diligent, committed study for spiritual growth and development resulting in intimate fellowship and relationship with God and our Saviour and Lord Jesus Christ is, and remains, the priority. I will be using some words that may offend some but are meant to describe some very apparent conditions that are alive, but are more sick than well, yet thriving and somewhat destructive, in humanity. God is much more of a gentleman than I am and limits his language to words such as fool, fools, and foolishness. I get a little rougher in my references to mankind and use words such as stupid, idiotic, ignorance etc.

Please understand I have nothing against people, only against the conditions listed above, stupidity, idiocy, and ignorance, etc, that humanity has such an overwhelming desire to wallow and remain in to the degradation of themselves, their societies, and nations, when God, in his love, has given us the remedy for deliverance from such nonsense. To refuse, or neglect, to avail oneself of what God has made available for deliverance from sin and its results in itself, puts a persons intelligence in question.

You are certainly welcome to disagree with me and raise an argument in protest if you wish, however, just a little understanding of the condition our nation is in and how it arrived at this state of demise from the abominations of sin and iniquity of its inhabitants should settle the argument and any questions about it once and for all.

I do hope to wake many minds that have gone to sleep to the challenge of some new in-depth thought that will project them into new ways of life and living where **"the heart is diligently kept, clean, and guarded" [Proverbs 4:23], the mind and spirit are renewed, [Romans 12: 2; Psalms 51:10], and the soul prospers" [3 John: 2].** If we continue to think the way we've always thought, we'll continue to get what we've always got. The way humanity is digressing, we cannot afford to continue along that road of demented mentality, either as individuals or as a nation.

It is my intention that other books will be written as the inspiration to do so presents itself. Several others are already in the works, all dealing with Biblical truths as they relate to the problems and dilemmas of our present day and time; all based on man's disobedience and rebellion against God. This has been the story down through the ages and has only intensified as the population of man has increased, **[Hosea 4: 7], "As they were increased, so they sinned against me: therefore I will change their glory into shame".** It is this increase in intensity of disobedience, rebellion, sin, iniquity, etc, etc, call it what you will, that has proven so disastrous to mankind that prompts

8

referral to the conditions of stupidity, idiocy, and ignorance with which man has so chosen to characterize himself.

It is the overabundance of these things that has brought such confusion and chaos to our nation and indeed the world. We could work our way through some of it, but when it became the norm of mankind's mentality and conduct, we have become overwhelmed by it, and can no longer see a light at the end of the tunnel, so to speak. The problems have not changed thru the ages, but remain internal, in the mentalities of some of **"our own countrymen"** who have formed alliances against the Bible, its teachings, and those who teach it. As a result, our leaders are frustrated, the news media is frustrated, and consequently the people are driven to frustration, and confusion seems to reign supreme, especially in the ranks of the people who have rejected God's word of truth and absolutes.

I will refrain from opening any argument as to whether or not the redeemed community of Christ are any better than the unsaved, as **[John 3: 16]** points out that Christ died for all, of which we were all qualified as ungodly, **[Romans 3: 23], " For all have sinned and come short of the glory of God"**. I am willing to leave that distinction between the saved and unsaved up to God as he separates the sheep from the goats, as who qualifies as a sheep versus a goat is entirely up to him, **[Matthew 25: 32].** In the meantime, however we might consider **[Acts 10: 34-35]** as a point of interest and consideration by those who have eyes to see, ears to hear, and minds that are capable of comprehension and at least a little bit of understanding; **"Then Peter open his mouth and said, of a truth I perceive that God is no respecter of persons: BUT in every nation he that feareth him, and worketh righteousness, is accepted with him"**.

Having favor with God through meeting his Biblical directed requirements for such favor, and being accepted with him is a very comforting, and intelligent, position to be in. You may well get away with disagreeing with me, but to disagree with God will have some eternal devastating affects: I would suggest a path more in line with God's choosing. I would offer **[Deuteronomy 30: 19]** for intense consideration and study for beginners and as a refresher for the more advanced students, or just readers, of the Bible.

Please don't get me wrong: I am not down on America, only the stupidity and ignorance that is bringing about her ruin, and the idiots that promote and practice it; which is all within their "rights" of course. God created us to be intelligent beings, however, Adam cast that aside when he abdicated his dominion authority to Satan in the Garden of Eden, and man has been abdicating every since. Retained and exercised Godly intelligence would prevent the things that are bringing ruination, shame, and disgrace on our beloved America, but Godly intelligence and common sense seem to be non-existent in our nation these days along with other things mentioned in the Bible that are commensurate with righteous and holiness.

The question of, who is to blame, should prompt some interesting discussion and dialogue. Who knows, during the process, we might even discover the solution to many of our problems. As Christians, that should already be quite apparent. **[Isaiah 5: 24], "Therefore as the fire devoureth the stubble, and the flame consumeth the chaff, so their root shall be as rottenness, and their flower shall go up as the dust: BECAUSE they have cast away the law of the Lord of hosts, and despised the word of the Holy One of Israel".** The first portion of this scripture gives us a fair description of America if we don't get our spiritual act together. The latter portion gives us the result of excommunicating God and His Word by such things as "the separation of the church and state".

Then we have the remedy, **[Mark 1: 15]**, **"Repent and believe the gospel unto diligent obedience.** This is a repeat of **[2 Chronicles 7: 14]**, **"If my people, which are called by my name, shall humble themselves, and pray, and seek my face, and turn from their wicked ways;** *then* **I will hear from heaven, and will forgive their sin, and will heal their land"**. There are a few more words used to emphasize this repentance essential, but the message is the same. **[Deuteronomy 28]** gives a very graphic difference between the people who dwell on the **"If thou wilt hearken diligently"** side of God's directions versus the unrepentant, **"If thou wilt not hearken diligently"** side in rebellion and disobedience. Consider this carefully.

Lacking the extended education that many of today's authors have, you may find my writings a bit rough around the edges for which I make no apology. This could prove an advantage in some ways as I don't have some things to unlearn as I progress and move ahead in my own studies. However, if we all stay with the same Bible for the purpose of unity, **[John 17],** and, to put in today's vernacular, "being on the same page", worshipping and serving the same God, creator of heaven and earth, the God of Israel, and diligently adhering to His counsel, we should remain fairly accurate as we progress, **"seated together in heavenly places in Christ"**, **[Ephesians 2: 4-10]**, continuing toward our eternal destiny of the kingdom of heaven while **[Deuteronomy 28: 47]**, **"serving the Lord our God with joyfulness, and with gladness of heart for the abundance of all things"**.

Though it seems that I may ramble a bit from time to time, it is my intention, whether I succeed or not, to present the readers with some Biblical truths and challenges they can get their "spiritual teeth into" for the purpose of growth, and development that they can apply toward Christian maturity, providing they are interested in doing so. If they are not so inclined, it is my prayer that some of these writings will induce enough curiosity to provide a challenge to compel them to additional studies, with my own writings and a multitude of others that are available to them. Let me challenge you to choose the books you read, and study, with wisdom and discretion, selecting only those that **"add something to you"** in the way of developing a Biblical, Christ like character, personality and attitude, **"with the Word of God dwelling in you richly", [Colossians 3: 15-17], vs. 16.**

You may find an occasional word misspelled for which I do apologize. Nevertheless, my main concern is that it is not misspelled so badly that it fails to contribute constructively to the message it is intended to convey. Allow me to assume my readers will have enough grace to overlook my errors and enough intelligence to get over the rough spots and around the chuck holes and capture the essence of these writings. May God richly bless you as you graciously walk with me through my efforts to present God's truth and absolutes to you for counsel, guidance, and direction unto life and life more abundantly, giving glory, honor, and pleasure, to God, magnifying our Saviour Jesus, and edifying the body of Christ.

Although I am a fan of the Kings James Version, which I will use in the majority of my writing, I will not hesitate to refer to other Versions from time to time as occasionally I will find a word or phrase that seems more preferable to what needs to be said in order to get a better understanding of the message being given. An attempt will be made to identify the use of these various scriptures from the different versions with an explanation of why they are being used in preference to the K.J.V. By doing this it is hoped we can "stay on the same page".

You will notice the use of much scripture throughout my writing with several scriptures being used many times in various situations. You may criticize this as redundancy if you wish. We were all born critics and man has developed it to a fine art, whether it be constructive or destructive, which it is in most cases as man has only to allow his nature to take its natural course to do this. However, what some may view as redundancy in the often use and application of Biblical truths, I simply see as **"emphasis"** to be diligently applied as needed substance for Christian character and development in all our lives. May God give you additional understanding of his word every time you come into contact with it. May it be often and consistent; for emphasis and effect, of course.

As a conclusion to this introduction, allow me once again to go to the scriptures, **[Hebrews 13: 20-21], "Now the God of peace, that brought again from the dead our Lord Jesus, that great shepherd of the sheep, through the everlasting covenant, Make you perfect in every good work to do his will, working in you that which is well pleasing in his sight, through Jesus Christ; to whom be glory for ever and ever. Amen.** I look forward to meeting you in heaven, and possibly before.

Sincerely, in God's love
Darold F. Edwards

NOTES

NOTES

ii.   # ACKNOWLEDGMENTS

I would like to thank the people who from the very beginning as a novice writer were kind enough to read some of my earliest efforts and gave me some very encouraging reviews. First of course I would like to thank God for guiding me into writing. It has become a real Godsend to me and has provided direction and purpose for me at a time when otherwise, retirement could have been very trying. I need purpose in my life and writing of the nature you will see in these books gave me that. During my electrical career when I was able to help build some material churches, I thought that someday I would like to assist in building the spiritual church in the hearts and lives of people. God has opened the door to do that through writing for which I wish to express my soul depth gratitude.

Next, many heartfelt thanks to my dear wife Pat for encouraging me in everything along the way in our life together, what a strength and help she has been to me. Susan Canfield was one of the first, who has been very encouraging from the start. She also trims our Schnauzer, Max, which is another big help. This doesn't really have anything to do with my writing except it provides opportunity to visit with Susan from time to time to get additional input on the writing; she is always encouraging. Susan has been very helpful and encouraging in her comments and friendship. Thank you Susan.

Then there is Jock and Karen Elliot, some dear Christian friends who along with their family we have been blessed to know for many reasons including their encouragement in writing. Karen is also a great cook, which is another real advantage to knowing the right people, and I have been much blessed in this area by her talent. My son Myke is of an absolute necessity and blessing as he is my computer expert along with being my son and a very dear friend. I couldn't do this without him. Thanks Myke, for your ever patient and loving assistance along the way.

Then there is my dear friend and brother in the Lord, Clarence Parker, who comes over a couple of times a week just to talk, discuss, study Bible, and add his encouragement to me in my writing efforts. His comments are extremely uplifting and helpful.   He also benefits from Karen's cooking, as do all who attend the Elliot's prayer meetings. What a great blessing and strength he is. Thank you my brother for standing alongside me during my writing struggles. Another dear friend, Nancy Gerling, has read some of my writings and has copies of my first efforts to have books published. She has always been extremely uplifting with her input concerning my writing. Many thanks to you, Nancy.

There are others that have added much to me with their encouraging comments about my works which are much appreciated. May God's blessings be upon them and may his presence fill their hearts and lives. May God's blessings also be added to you who are gracious enough to become a part of my reading public; let us study God's word together as he quickens us together in Christ, raises us up together, and makes us to sit together in heavenly places in Christ Jesus our Lord and Saviour, these places being made heavenly because of His presence, wherever that may be. May God's divine love abound in our hearts toward one another. Indeed; we do become a part of each other as we are a part of the body of Christ our Lord.

A little over a year ago as I was looking through a magazine advertising for a Restore America event, I run across another page where someone made the statement, **"How much information do we need before we get out of the boat and walk on the water"**. Whoever that person is, and wherever he may be, I would like to thank him for impacting my life with that inspirational word. Stepping out in faith and writing as I feel led of the Lord in my efforts is my way of walking on the water.

Your efforts are probably of a different calling than mine, but yet of the divine nature. May we blend our efforts and lives together in the unity Jesus prayed for in **John 17** for God's glory, honor, and pleasure. Come, walk with me as we journey along together with the multitudes who will join with us, as we all walk and sit together **"in heavenly places"**, inspiring each other as Jesus inspires us all. **To God be the glory forever and ever, Amen.**

NOTES

iii.   **PREFACE**

[Ecclesiastes 12: 11-12], "The words of the wise are as goads, and as nails fastened by the masters of the assemblies, which are given from one Shepard. And further, by these, my son, be admonished: of making many books there is no end; and much study is a weariness to the flesh". Much study demands considerable self discipline, diligence and determination, and a lot of invested time, whereas simply reading for the enjoyment of what is being read, or other lesser purposes, without the element of **"study to show thyself approved unto God", [2 Timothy 2: 15],** tends to a great waste of time.

However, such is not the case if a time of relaxation from business or other things that tend to stress is needed, and reading a good book that is a "no brainer" may be just the ticket. Unfortunately this becomes the norm for many people. As a result many books that neither contribute anything of value and add nothing constructive to the readers, are in great abundance, and offer no challenge for growth and development. Consequently no study is required that would demand thought and concentration, so these books are read in pursuit of nothing, then put aside in favor of another "nothing" book or maybe just watching soap operas on T.V. or the equivalent in "nothing". Habits are thus formed with the result being wasted time and life.

Allow me to express extreme caution in the selection of your reading material as your reading is a direct input into the content of your mind and contributes heavily to "the abundance of your heart". So once again I say, proceed with wisdom, knowledge, understanding, and caution, applying some intelligence and plain common sense along the way, **[Proverbs**

4: 23], **"Keeping thy heart with all diligence; for out of it are the issues of life".** [Proverbs 2: 11], **"Discretion shall preserve thee; understanding shall keep thee".**

If we do not endeavor to establish our values and standards according to God's values and standards, we will exist in error continually without the life God has made available to us through Jesus Christ. It is with this in mind that I have set out to produce this work concerning the "RESURRECTION OF EXCELLENCY", to challenge the readers, whoever or wherever they may be: to look inside themselves and ask intelligent questions about their being, who they are, what they are, how they came to be, their purpose, and what their eternal destiny is, and what it is comprised of and by God's design. I find it very enlightening to realize I have by "intelligent design" been created as a very special and unique being instead as a blob of something left to chance as claimed by some who are also willing to risk their eternal destiny with their continuing low level of an unchallenged demented mentality.

Don't think me uncaring and insensitive to others because I use words such as stupidity, idiocy, and ignorant at times. We have all been there and if we are not careful and conscientious about our Christian training, have a tendency to revert back to old habits from time to time. I have nothing against man; only against the inadequate mentalities they have chosen to victimize themselves with. Even as Christians, former erroneous habits and desires, at times even with God's assistance, are hard to shake and it takes time, perseverance and diligence to cast them aside and grow out of them. They may or may not be classified as sin in all cases, but regardless consist of things that do not **"please the Lord," [John 8: 29], or "accompany salvation," [Hebrews 6: 9].** But in any event we need to **[2 Timothy 2: 15], "Study to show ourselves approved unto God, workmen that needeth not to be ashamed, rightly dividing the word of truth."** This involves the extensive effort of   **[Romans 12: 2]**

"being transformed by the renewing of the mind", **"exercising thyself unto Godliness"**, [1 Timothy 4: 7].

The displacing of these life destroying discrepancies will only be accomplished with the diligent study and input of God's Word. These are just simply some destructive traits of humanity that if not addressed and dealt with according to God's counsel, will continue to plague their unsuspecting, unknowledgeable victims regardless of whether or not they are saved. The devil is not choosey who he victimizes and he will use any method at his disposal to re-devour anyone who becomes negligent in the **"keeping of the heart with all diligence"**, **[Proverbs 4: 23].** Remember, as a Christian, you are his prime target, you are his priority. All others are already devoured. Such is the result of disregarding God's counsel and direction to **"choose life and blessing rather than death and cursing" [Deuteronomy 30: 19].**

I have had to reject the traditional terminology of "sinner saved by grace" in favor of **"a new creature in Christ, saved by Grace", [2 Corinthians 5: 17].** The reason for this was because the term "sinner" was not conducive to being **[1 John 1: 7-9], "forgiven of sin and cleansed from all unrighteousness by the blood of Jesus."** This is an insult to the power of the blood of Jesus to thoroughly cleanse from sin and unrighteousness in the name of Jesus for complete cleansing, forgiveness, deliverance and reconciliation. All this of course, is based on the condition of genuine, soul depth, repentance of sin and a commitment to **"fear [reverence] the Lord and work righteousness" [Acts 10: 35], serving the Lord with joyfulness and with gladness of heart, for the abundance of all things, [Deuteronomy 28: 47].** You may not agree with me on this issue and that's not important. Just be in agreement with God. It's his word that counts, not mine.

After all that God has done for us through Jesus Christ our Lord and Saviour in obtaining the **"divine nature of God through his great and precious promises", [2 Peter 1:2 -4],** it seemed that the title and name of "sinner" had some rather antagonistic and invasive qualities and connotations about it that never belonged nor fit in well with being "a new creature in Christ saved by grace". The term "sinner" always suggested being stuck in a rut with no incentive to move on, whereas the new distinction and a new attitude concerning being "a new creature in Christ" provides a glorious challenge to, **[1 Peter 1: 13], "Gird up the loins of our [spiritual] minds"** and, **[Hebrews 6: 1-3], "go on unto perfection",** to the **[Job 4: 21], "Resurrection of the Excellency" which is in you, lest ye die, even without wisdom."**

NOTES

____

____

____

____

____

____

____

____

____

____

I.   FRUIT OF THE SPIRIT

[2 Peter 1:2-13] Grace and peace be multiplied unto you through the knowledge of God, and of Jesus our Lord. According as his divine power hath given unto us all things that pertain unto life and godliness, through the knowledge of him that hath called us to glory and virtue: Whereby are given unto us exceeding great and precious promises: that by these ye might be "partakers" of the DIVINE NATURE, having escaped the corruption that is in the world through lust.

Bits and pieces of the next few verses, along with other portions of scripture from various parts of the Bible, will be referred to as we go along to add to the "Fruit of the Spirit" as we explore this "Divine Nature" of God. It is his intention and desire, it would seem, for us to be partakers of, and apply, these **[Hebrews 6:9], "things that accompany salvation"** along with other things found in **[2 Peter 1:5-7]**, which may well be considered also as "fruit of the Spirit" though not in the list of **[Galatians 5:22-23].** This is some additional exploration of this "creative" God and our Lord Jesus Christ in our search to discover new areas of growth and attainment awaiting us as we, **[Hebrews 6:1], "go on unto perfection"** to teach us and lead us into what we were initially meant to be like, **[John 14: 26], "But the Comforter, which is the Holy Ghost, whom the Father will send in my name, he will teach you all things, and bring to your remembrance, whatsoever I have said unto you.**

This is all contributive to the "Resurrection of Excellency", both learning, accumulating, and sharing, of the knowledge that prevents destruction, **[Hosea 4:6].** Some of the, lifestyle, with contents of the "excellency" contained in the "likeness" of this "divine nature" are contained in these next few verses given in **chapter one of 2 Peter: they are vs.5, diligence, faith, virtue,**

knowledge, vs.6, temperance, patience, godliness, vs.7, brotherly kindness, and charity. Throughout Psalms and Proverbs in various scriptures we find exhortation to learn and exercise **wisdom, knowledge, understanding, discretion, and again we are reminded to use diligence in attaining to, possessing, and doing these things.** All the above mentioned things that are characteristic of the "divine nature" can well be considered as additional to, and supportive of, the list of "things" we have in: **[Galatians 5:22-23], " The FRUIT of the SPIRIT, love, joy, peace, longsuffering, gentleness, goodness, faith, meekness, and temperance".**

We can get a brief look here into the divine nature of God, but a brief look is all we can expect until we devote some time and effort in the study of these and other things that will become apparent as we maintain diligence in our study habits. Beyond the knowledge that these things that are available for us in our journey into the, relatively unknown, divine nature of God, is the **studying, learning and practicing** of these things. This is for the purpose of application, exercising, and blending our lives with them for the overall, explicit purpose of bringing glory and honour to God, and **[John 8:29] doing always those "things" that please him.** Our lifestyles must be characterized by the presence and exercising of these "things".

When you come to the word "*things*", don't take it lightly for there is a lifetime of study to be done within the confines of "things" which we find referred to in many scriptures including **[Hebrews 6:9], "the better "*things*" that accompany salvation".** A great many of them are used in reference to, and in connection with, the application of the "Resurrection of Excellency" contained in the image and likeness of God. We are the beneficiaries of this whole program of redemption and reconciliation that almighty God has designed and made available for us through Jesus Christ our Lord, and Saviour.

We must study and *"get a vision of the value"* of these "things", with the benefits and rewards alluded to in **[Hebrews 11:6], "for without faith it is impossible to please him: for he that cometh to God must believe that he is, and that he is a REWARDER of them that DILIGENTLY seek him"**. We can find another direct reference, there are others, to these "things" in **[Deuteronomy 28:47], for the willing, loving obedience to God, "*Because* thou servedst the Lord thy God with joyfulness and gladness of heart for the *abundance of all "things"*.** It would, without a doubt, appear that God wants us to avail ourselves of all that he has made available to us throughout the whole Biblical program of salvation, redemption, and reconciliation through Christ Jesus our Lord and Saviour. Whether we do or not is entirely up to us as individuals.

Our lives, by necessity, must show signs and characteristics of the *"Fruit of the Spirit"* **[works meet for repentance, Acts 26: 20]** and **[fruits meet for repentance, Matthew 3: 8],** in our pursuit of the "divine nature", rather than the continued signs and characteristics of this world of sin we are in, but not of. This is a world we are mentally, spiritually, and physically departing from as our knowledge of, and intimacy with, God increases and intensifies. *Mentally,* because we are learning to think and have thoughts more like God's thoughts through the **study of [2 Timothy 2:15], delighting and meditation of [Psalms 1:2], and [Romans 12:2] unto the renewing of our minds;** *spiritually,* because we are learning to make the distinctions between the Holy Spirit and the moving of God versus the evil, contrary, anti Bible, anti Christ influences of this world; *physically,* because we are called and learning to **[Romans 12:1] "present our bodies as a living sacrifice unto God, which is our reasonable service".**

The intended result is our conduct becoming considerably upgraded from what it used to be, **[Ephesians 2:1-3],** as we *"turn from our wicked ways"* and enjoy the results in **verses 4-10,** depending of course on our **diligence of study and application** of what is learned along the way, and enjoying the results of peace gained and established throughout the whole process, **[1 Peter 3: 10-11], For he that will love life, and see good days, let him refrain his tongue from evil, and his lips that they speak no guile: Let him eschew evil, and do good; let him** *seek peace and ensue it".* This is the process of being transformed out of an existence of the darkness of this world into the light and life of the "kingdom of God" by the renewing of our minds unto the gospel truths of God's Word. We have a long ways to go, but bless God we are learning, sometimes from the bumps on the other fellows head, or if we are not intelligent enough to do it that way, from the bumps on our own head. Sometimes we are not even intelligent enough to learn this way, but keep repeating the same stupid mistakes over and over again with more resultant lumps. *Stupidity may not always consist of sinful things, but indulgence in sin is always stupid.*

Preferably, however, our learning comes from diligent study and application of whatever is gleaned from God's Word. If we will exercise ourselves to learn to think right according to Biblical counsel, our ways will have a tendency to take on an aura of correctness also. Turning from our wicked ways is of extreme importance, but is only one of the four ingredients of repentance found in **[2 Chronicles 7: 14].** This principle of repentance fits individuals as well as nations and is definitely intended to be applied and exercised by both.

This all begins with a "choice", a soul depth repentance of all that is contrary to God's Word, moving on unto the maturity of "Christ likeness of the divine nature", **[2 Peter 1: 4],** *and doing always those things that please God* **[John 8: 29],** *his thinking, his thoughts, and thus his ways* **[Isaiah 55: 8-9],** passing from death unto life, from darkness into light, **[John 5: 24].** Thus do we learn **[Isaiah 28:10], "line upon line, precept**

upon precept, here a little, and there a little". We advance three steps, begin to slide back, take a few lumps and stop at two and one half, but in the process we gained a half step. God picks us up, dusts us off with his amazing grace; we **"stir ourselves up to take a better hold on him" [Isaiah 64:7],** and with renewed determination and diligence from the half step gained, give it another try with a smile on our face and gratitude in our hearts for his grace and assistance in the overall process of the half step gained.

We will, we have, and we are in the process of **[Romans 8:37], being "more than conquerors through him that loved us", and continues to love us.** And so we continue to learn, **"doing the word", being cleansed by its application [John 15:3],** and manifesting it's teaching in daily living, in and through our relationships with others. **[Matthew 25:40] "And the King shall answer and say unto them, Verily I say unto you, Inasmuch as ye have done it unto the least of these my brethren, ye have done unto me. As you would have others do unto you, do ye also unto them."**

America is obsessed with physical exercise to attempt to attain to some standard of acceptable body condition, however the idea of developing the mentality into that which is acceptable to God and beneficial to all, including ourselves, never seems to be a consideration and an essential part of the thought process. **[1Timothy 4:7-8], "Exercise thyself rather unto godliness, for bodily exercise profiteth little: but godliness is profitable unto all things, having promise of the life that now is, and of that which is to come."** Man is influenced, conditioned, and intimidated to move mentally and physically within the limits of what he has been conditioned to by the general world situations that surround him.

Learn to think outside the abnormal world influencing of subtle unrighteousness of **[Hebrews 12:1], "the sin that so**

easily besets us", unto the Biblical counsel of God-likeness, beginning with the [Mark 1:15], cleansing of repentance, believing, and doing the gospel of truth". This is all a part of the accepting of this King of righteousness and holiness, Jesus as Saviour and Lord, for deliverance from all the past that would lure you into a destructive future. Instead you are introduced to the truth that leads you into the realization of **"life and life more abundantly", [John 10: 10].** This is a life of promise, provision, progression, blessings, and peace, as we learn to **"do always those things that please God" and do them [Deuteronomy 28:47], "with joyfulness and gladness of heart for the abundance of all things."**

The sin [Hebrews 12:1], "which doth so easily beset us" *is not a "given"* just because we live in a world that is filled with it, **[John 15:19; 17:14],** for we are not of this world, but are of God's kingdom of victory and righteousness that dwells within us through Jesus Christ our Lord. We live in a physical, material world that was beautifully created by God, but because of the sinful world within it that man has created for himself; God's whole creation has been adversely affected and corrupted by that sin. Satan was certainly the one who introduced this program, when as Lucifer in **[Ezekiel 28:15], "iniquity was found in thee",** and man became a deceived but willing player on his team of rebellion, iniquity and abomination against God every since. As a result, man has been wallowing in sin as a hog wallows in mud every since and dragged God's creation in with him. However, I have decided, as Jesus gave me a way out, not to participate in this stupidity wherein once, I to, found pleasure **[Ephesians 2:1-3]** as an idiot and willing participant.

There is absolutely no comparison in the momentary, physical, and emotional pleasures of the sins of this world with the eternal peace of mind, heart and soul that are a result of **[Acts 17:28], "living and moving and having your being in Christ".** **"But God, [Ephesians 2: 4-10], who is rich in**

mercy, for his great love wherein he loved us, even when we were dead in sins, hath quickened us together with Christ, [by grace are ye saved:] and hath raised us up together, and made us sit together in heavenly places in Christ Jesus; that in, and throughout, ages to come he might show his exceeding riches of his grace in his kindness toward us through Christ Jesus." We must learn what is in this world that is not of this world but is in fact, of God and make the distinction and separation of the two in thought and practice, **"setting our affection on the things above and not on the things on the earth",[Colossians 3:2].** Sex, for instance, is not a creation of this world, however, the non-Biblical misuse and perversion of it is. Proper sexual relationships are Biblically taught and ordained of God within the marriage of a man and woman, not the same sex perversion that is being imposed by the minds of iniquity and abomination unto acceptance in today's society. Such practices and indulgences are graphically contributive to bringing God's judgment on the guilty parties and societies of such lifestyles. **[Mark 1: 15], "Repent and believe the gospel unto obedience".**

The degradation of sin and filth knows no bounds, but continues to sink to lower depths as man continues in **[Romans 1:30], his "inventions of evil things".** [Luke 6:45] **"A good man out of the good treasure of his heart bringeth forth that which is good; and an evil man out of the evil treasure of his heart bringeth forth that which is evil; for of the abundance of the heart his mouth speaketh." [Out of the abundance of the heart the mind thinks, the mouth speaks, and the body does, and none of us are exempt or immune from the temptations thereof.] Our prevailing mentality is either deliverance unto life, or a sentence of death, it leads and we, like sheep, follow. Man needs a renewing of his mind, his mentality, his thinking.** Once again **[Isaiah 55: 8-9]** applies.

There is no end to what is to be learned, practiced, and initiated in the realm of God's kingdom, **[Matthew 6:33],** that dwells within you as a practicing Christian and seeking his righteousness. We must all exercise ourselves to get our mentalities locked into this **"Kingdom of God" [Acts17:28] living, and moving, and having our being, mentally, spiritually, and physically in him.** We will not live, and, move, and have our being in this kingdom of holiness and righteousness physically until we obey God's word and at least begin **[Isaiah 28:10],** this process of being transformed out of this world of iniquity and sin by the **"renewing of our minds unto Biblical counsel and direction",** **[Romans 12: 2].** As we "diligently" involve ourselves in the process of this renewing transformation of our mentalities, we will progressively embrace the spiritual aspect of this renewing process and begin to really see the importance of *"getting a vision of the value"* of an ever greater and stronger intimacy with God.

Bear in mind that as soon as you "repent and believe the gospel" with the diligence and intensity needed for the results required, **[Romans 10:9] confessing with the mouth and believing in the heart,** you will be as saved as you can ever be. However this being saved, born again, washed in the blood of Jesus, is an introduction into, and registration in God's program of "higher education", his school house, and it begins with, by necessity, very elementary teaching. It starts in **[Hebrews 5:12-14], "the milk of the Word for the babes,** and over time, patience, and much study and practice, progresses **to the strong meat of the Word for the mature.**

Passage of time does not, however, guarantee a person's spiritual maturity. It is what they do during that passage of time that makes the difference. Faithful church attendance does not guarantee spiritual growth and development. A person does not become a **"new creature"** by being in church, but by **"being in Christ", [2 Corinthians 5: 17].** We can only hope that whatever church a person is attending will greatly facilitate such growth and development. It is not only the responsibility of the church leaders to make sure the means for this are available, but also to the individuals to avail themselves of such means as provided, whether by qualified teachers or their own personal Bible exploration and study. All the best teacher can do is teach, it is up to you to do the learning and application of what is presented. We all do, as followers, bear the responsibility of being diligent followers of that which is according to holiness and righteousness in preparation of becoming future leaders. This is vitally essential for whatever position or capacity of leadership in which we find ourselves, from being a parent, which is the most important, to being a president. We must at all times and under all circumstances keep our focus and **"affection set on things above, and not on things on earth", [Colossians 3: 2].**

Please do not misunderstand me; the church even with its faults when man gets in God's way for the operation and administration, is still the only institution on this earth that provides instruction in God's affairs of righteousness and holiness. No doubt Jesus himself was aware of the frailty and failure of humans in this respect when he announced in **[Matthew 16: 18],** that he was going to build his own church, **"against which these gates of hell, failures and weaknesses, would not prevail".** I wish all people everywhere attended church and Sunday-school; I also wish that ever church and Sunday-school attended would provide, present, and effectively teach that which is required by God's own standard, the spiritual food necessary for the spiritual growth needed for maturity. Unfortunately this is not the case. **[Psalms 127: 1], "Except the Lord build the house, they labor in vain that build it: except the Lord keep the city, the watchman waketh but in vain". [1 Corinthians 3: 11], "For other foundation can no man lay than that is laid, which is Jesus Christ".** It is on this **foundational rock,** this **"sure**

foundation", [Isaiah 28:16], that Jesus is today, building his house, his church.

Most of us, myself included, come into this family of God dumber than a stick about spiritual things. However, if the process develops and progresses as God intends it should, these dumb dead sticks take on **a newness of life and develop into beautiful, good fruit bearing trees: [Psalms 1:3], [Proverbs 11:30], [John 14:26].** The Holy Spirit is the teacher and the Holy Bible is the textbook. YOU are the student. Now let us hope you progress at least as rapidly and with the grades you expect and desire of your own children in their earthly schools of lower and elementary education as they proceed to "higher education".

Unfortunately both of these schools have dropouts as well as those who, regardless of the expertise of teaching and material provided, just do not apply themselves. Let's face it, if our young people don't progress any faster in their secular training as some of us as adults do in our spiritual training its no wonder that parents get a bit perplexed from time to time. After all, our kids are under a bit of a handicap as they are expected to progress in both secular and spiritual education at the same time. What a wonderful thing that quite a large number of them do. But it's a tragedy that an even larger number of them don't. This, however, could be said about the adult population also. Thank God for the exceptions that he continues to raise up, both young and older. It is, however, more difficult to swim against a current of opposition to Godliness than it is to just drift along in the current of conformity to it, wherein we were all born. We certainly need God's assistance to do this, and do it successfully.

The tragedy of this situation in the world is, that it requires very little time, little effort, no knowledge and absolutely no wisdom or intelligence to produce young and multitudes of them are produced on a consistent basis. They are produced without wisdom, knowledge, understanding, and certainly without intelligence or common sense, or for that matter any other of Biblical requirements even entering into the picture until it's to late and in many families, never. But with God, all things are possible, and as long as there is life, there is hope and that hope is found only in this living God of hope who [2 Peter 1:2-4], **"according to his divine power hath given unto us all things that pertain to life and godliness, through the knowledge of him that hath called us to glory and virtue: Whereby are given unto us exceeding great and precious promises: that by these ye might be partakers of the divine nature, having escaped the corruption that is in the world through lust."**

In the next three verses of, **2 Peter, verses 5, 6, & 7,** we find a list of things we need to add to and even include with the **"fruit of the spirit" of Gal. 5:22-23,** for they are indeed additional "fruit". Two of them, **faith and temperance**, are on both lists with others having similar meanings such as **longsuffering and patience, love and charity,** but all characteristics of the "divine nature", blend together and support each other. We need to include [2 Peter 1: 10] here for the exhortation contained therein: **"Wherefore the rather, brethren, give diligence to make your calling and election sure: for if ye DO THESE THINGS, ye shall never fall".** "Doing these things" is an absolute necessity. Please understand; this verse 10 is much more than a mere suggestion or exhortation from God, but takes on the form of a commandment or to take it a bit farther, a law, or an established "principle".

Call it whatever you are comfortable with that contributes to your "divine nature' attainment. Regardless, however, GIVE DILIGENCE to these things listed above along with the "Fruit of the Spirit", **the things that please God, [John 8:29], and**

the things that accompany salvation, [Hebrews 6:9]. GIVE DILIGENCE to these things in order to make your calling and election sure: for if you don't do these things, you have already fallen in disobedience and rebellion against God. The grace of God is a wonderful gift and provision of God; don't forfeit it with stupidity and idiocy. It was never intended to replace obedience or allow disobedience.

I have a friend, Jim Justus; that has a saying that fits in well here. "You gotta learn to pay attention". Pick your Bible up and read it, study it: *that's God talking: pay attention.* **[2 Timothy 3:16], "All scripture is given by inspiration of God, and is profitable for doctrine, for reproof, for correction, for instruction in righteousness: vs. 17 that the man of God may be perfect, thoroughly furnished unto all good works".** PAY ATTENTION, **[Jeremiah 12:11], layeth it to heart, [Job 4:20], regard it, [Malachi 2:2]; hear it, [Psalms 1: 2] delight in it and meditate on it. Your eternity and that of your "seed", your children, your descendents, [Deuteronomy 30:19],** *depends on it.* PAY ATTNTION! Don't get sidetracked on the subject of grace here; that has its own application. These are laws, principles, and counsel that God, in his wisdom, knowledge, understanding, and intelligence has given us for our own benefit, our growth, maturity development, and fruitfulness in his kingdom, because of his love and grace: **"the better things that accompany salvation and always please God";** whereby, **[3 John 1:2], "our souls may prosper and as a result we may prosper and be in health". PAY ATTENTION!**

Now let's discuss these "things" that for the most part, have fallen through the cracks, and because of this, **[Job 4:20], "They are destroyed from morning to evening: they perish for ever, continually, without any regarding it,** "PAY ATTENTION". Starting with the "Fruit of the Spirit", the first one is: LOVE, or CHARITY as used in **[1 Corinthians 13]**

K.J.V. It seems that LOVE and CHARITY are used interchangeably, depending on the different versions and the translators involved. It does make it a bit difficult to keep everyone on the same page when you may find several different versions being used at the same time by different people in the same service or Bible study etc. I know from personal experience that it can create confusion and difference of opinions that detract from the unity necessary for harmony in the family of God that must be maintained regardless of our personal feelings and emotions. Furthermore, if we have personal feelings and emotions that are out of harmony with God's will and desires, a re-evaluation of our relationship with Jesus Christ must be considered. Love demands this but then again, there are a lot of people that don't understand love from God's viewpoint.

This is certainly something we all are learning, sometimes with great difficulty, and slowly. Love takes on many meanings depending on the situations and people involved with their various attitudes, ideas, and concepts formed over the years, whether good or bad, right or wrong, or in today's world; legal or illegal. At this point let us consider, once again, a scripture in, **[Colossians 3:2], "Set your affection on things above, not on things on earth".** In consideration of the renewing of our minds, we can interchange the word "affection" with "mind or heart". This gives us additional application of the need for renewing our minds for the purpose of fixing or centering our mentalities, our reason for being, on the **"things" that always please God and the "better things" that accompany salvation.** There is a direct connection with our affection that is to be set on things above and this phenomenon we refer to as "love". It makes for interesting study and searching of the scriptures. Try it; you'll like it, especially if you are interested in the things God has provided for us **"that pertain to life and Godliness" [2Peter 1:3].** Keep a good dictionary handy, you'll find it invaluable in your study exploration.

We probably get our best overall description of the demands, operations, and applications of love from **[1 Corinthians 13]** than are available anywhere else. Finis Jennings Dake, gives us in his Kings James Version of the Holy Bible concerning the subject of love, what he terms as, 9 ingredients of divine, or AGAPE, love that make an interesting study in themselves. They are as follows:

1. Patience – love passive: no hurry; suffers long; bears, believes, hopes, and endures all things [vs. 4, 7]

2. Kindness – love in action: never acts rashly or insolently; not inconsistent, puffed up, or proud [vs. 4]

3. Generosity – love in competition: not envious or jealous [vs. 4]

4. Humility – love in hiding: no parade; no airs; works then retires [vs. 4]

5. Courtesy – love in society: does not behave unseemly; always polite; at home with all classes; never rude or discourteous [vs.5]

6. Unselfishness – love in essence: never selfish, sour, or bitter; seeks only good of others; does not retaliate or seek revenge [vs.5]

7. Good temper, attitude – love in disposition: never irritated; never resentful [vs.5]

8. Righteousness – love in conduct: hates sin; never glad when others go wrong; always gladdened by goodness to others; always slow to expose; always eager to believe the best; always hopeful, always enduring [vs. 6-7]

9. Sincerity – love in profession: never boastful and conceited; not a hypocrite; always honest; leaves no impression but what is strictly true; never self-assertive; does not blaze out in passionate anger, nor brood over wrong; always just, joyful, and truthful; knows how to be silent; full of trust; always present.

There are generally two Greek words, agape and phileo, that are referred to in the Bible, agape being the more in depth and sincere while phileo being less intense and more shallow. There are many variations of both of these, which if a person desires a deeper and more complete understanding might consult a "Strong's Concordance with Hebrew and Greek Dictionaries. A person may attain to great knowledge and understanding of these things and still go through life with a considerable amount of difficulty attempting to sort out, and keep their own thoughts, feelings, emotions, attitudes, and resultant conduct contained in a manner that is pleasing to God. This teaching that Dake has provided for us will give anyone a good foundation on which to begin a thorough study of the attributes and applications of love and charity. May God bless you and enable you as you continue on your journey of "The Resurrection of Excellency" with "The Fruit of the Spirit".

There are many things that enter into the makeup of the "divine nature". I suppose we might even refer to them as the ingredients of the divine nature of God which we need to learn in order to initiate and incorporate into our lives for God's pleasure and certainly our own wellbeing. Bear in mind that as we learn to practice and exercise these things, we become the beneficiaries of the results. For instance, in the list of the **"Fruit of the Spirit in [Gal. 5:22-23], and an additional list in [2 Peter 1:5-7], we find such things as love, previously discussed, longsuffering, gentleness goodness, faith, meekness, and temperance. In the additional list in 2 Peter 1:5-7 we find diligence, faith, virtue, knowledge,**

38

temperance, patience, godliness, brotherly kindness, and charity, which may be identified as love, and is so used in some other translations.

The majority of the first list, and all of the additional are things that we learn to do, and some of them are contained in both list or have direct reference to each other in both lists, such as, longsuffering in the first list and patience in the second list, but nevertheless are things we need to learn, develop, and do in our lives. The other two remaining are in the first list, joy and peace. These are a direct result of our learning, embracing, and implementing all the others in our lives. One thing that is not included in these lists, there are others, is our thinking, **[Philippians 4:6-9], think on these things,** new thought processes, for a renewed, restructured, Bible based mentality. This is covered in **[Romans 12:1-2]** and sets the stage for everything else; vs. 2, **"Be not conformed to this world, but be ye transformed by the renewing of your mind, that ye may prove what is that good, and acceptable, and perfect will of God".**

This world knows nothing of the things contained in both lists pertaining to the divine nature, of the renewing of the mind unto conformity to God's word and will, of the wisdom, understanding, and the knowledge taught in Psalms and Proverbs in the Old Testament, nor of the Godly intelligence implied therein. *Is it any wonder this world is not experiencing this joy and peace that are a result of the practicing of the things that provide them.* As you think about these things God has provided for us and man's rejection of them, it is not hard to understand why this world is filled with wars, wars, rumors of wars, animosity, hatred, abominations of every sort, iniquity of every kind and description, etc, etc, etc, and etc. This is a principle that is present in an individual life, a nation, or the entire world, and we are witnessing it on our news media every time we turn on the news.

We live in nation, and indeed a world that has turned its back on God and despises his word and we and our children are paying a horrible price for it. It is amazing how many, supposedly intelligent people, refuse to acknowledge God, his word, and the Christian "religion" that is the foundation of the formation of this nation, but are quick to acknowledge him to blame him when things go wrong. One of my favorite quotations comes from Shakespeare and fits quite well here, **"What fools ye mortals be"**.

Now that I've done my ranting and raving about the arrows of stupidity and idiocy on which this world has impaled itself, lets return to some form of sanity concerning the "Fruit of the Spirit" and the accompanying scriptures. Concerning "love" as something we do, lets turn to **[Psalms 119:165]** as an example. **"Great peace have they which "do" LOVE thy law: and nothing shall offend, [or be a stumbling block to] them"**. From this we can see the necessity of "love" according to God's standards. It would help considerably if people can "get a vision of the value "of loving this law or "word of God" which is directly representative of God himself. **[Deuteronomy 30:20], "That thou mayest love the Lord thy God, and that thou mayest obey his voice, [his word], and that thou mayest cleave unto him: FOR HE IS THY LIFE, and the length of thy days"**. This should increase our desire and our ability to get a greater understanding of LOVE and its immense value and incorporate it into our lives. This would be a most intelligent thing for a person to do. If you have a desire to enjoy the **[Philippians 4:7], "peace of God that passes all understanding, and experience his [1Peter 1:8], joy unspeakable and full of glory"**, simply learn to do those things that always please HIM and enjoy his presence. Have a happy, prosperous, and fruitful journey in your quest for "The Resurrection of Excellency".

NOTES

II.   BIBLE PRINCIPLES MUST RULE

There must by necessity be a ruling entity, and that entity included, that is governed by an established set of principles that are and have been established to bring about the well being of all who subscribe to them and protect the subscribers and adherents of such a set of principles from all who do not subscribe, adhere to, and practice them. This set of principles must by necessity occupy the position referred to in **[Romans 13: 1]** as the **"higher powers"** to which **"every soul must be subject"** for the single mindedness of truth and righteousness that is of a necessity in order for man to live in unity and harmony as God intended he should within an orderly society. To elevate mere men to this exalted position of "higher powers", or allow this to happen, who have no regard or love for God and his principles of righteousness, His Word; is the height of stupidity and ignorance, and has proved to be disastrous. It will, is, and has, led to the formation of a world filled with disorderly, degraded nations and societies, including our own.

When God was excommunicated from our nation by the "separation of church and state" idiocy, the Godly condition of wisdom and intelligence went with him, and America has been groping in darkness every since. The erroneous rulings by our "leaders" against God, have adversely affected every man woman and child in our nation. These rulings have wreaked havoc among our institutions including our churches which should be declaring this set of Godly established divine rules and counsel of the Bible with unblemished commitment and boldness, unhindered, and undeterred by a hostile government that has shown bitter opposition to those God inspired and established principles of life and life more abundantly recorded within the scriptures.

Unfortunately our democratic government has shown itself to be among those that **honoureth God with their lips, but their heart is far from Him"**, **[Matthew 15: 8; Mark 7: 6]**. It is only fair to say that the majority not in governmental circles also qualify for this designation. Thank God for the exceptions that provide at least a semblance of order and decency in our nation, **[Matthew 16: 18], "Upon this rock of God revealed truth concerning who I am, *I* will build *my* church, and the gates of hell shall not prevail against *it*"**. The establishing and building of this church has nothing to do with Peter but has everything to do with Jesus Christ, the truth of who and what Jesus is as revealed by the Father and is manifested as considerably different from the multitude of churches man has attempted to build under his own efforts against which the gates of hell have prevailed and wreaked havoc. Once again, thank God for the exceptions.

Due to the majestic and good nature of these principles, and the complete temporal and eternal well being they have been designed to bring to all mankind; to violate them or any part of them is to be an enemy, **"opposing themselves", [2 Timothy 2: 25],** and all others of their species and the environment in which they live. Such violation, because of its leaven nature, will bring sure destruction to all who do not take special steps **[2 Chronicles 7: 14; Mark 1:15]** for deliverance and protection from the violators and the subtlety of their deceptive natures and resultant transgressions against God and the **"higher powers" of his divine nature, the abundance of his heart, His Word.**

This set of principles must have proved their viability, stability, supremacy, and value over all others that do not establish, provide for, and promote the well being of man, both temporal and eternal. This set of principles must have established their worthiness of supremacy throughout the history and experience of the existence of man through ages past with the sufficiency of proof and absolutes to believe and trust in their continuing truth which testifies to their consistency of sovereignty. This worthiness and supremacy confirms the right of the provider of this set of principles to be loved, honored, worshipped, and joyfully obeyed with a willing heart and mind.

No lesser being has any right, though the opportunities may be many, to violate these principles or the right of the God who established them to be worshipped, honored, loved, obeyed, and glorified. Only on these principles is it possible for peoples and nations to be established and prosper. We certainly have ample proof of their violation and the horrific results of such violation in our world today. And still man shows a complete lack of intelligence by his transgressions. **[Isaiah 5: 13-16], "Therefore my people are gone into captivity, because they have no knowledge: and their honorable men are famished, and their multitudes are dried up with thirst. Therefore hell hath enlarged herself, and opened her mouth without measure: and their glory, and their multitude, and their pomp, and he that rejoiceth, *shall descend into it.* And the mean man shall be brought down, and the mighty man shall be humbled, and the eyes of the lofty shall be humbled: BUT the Lord of hosts shall be exalted in judgment, and God that is holy shall be sanctified in righteousness". [Mark 12: 30], "And thou shalt love the Lord with all thy heart, and with all thy soul, and with all thy mind, and with all thy strength: this is the first [and great] commandment".**

This set of principles when applied and exercised must guarantee that this, "well being", will include and basically consist of, but not limited to, the "Fruit of the Spirit" as set forth in the Bible in the book of **[Galatians 5:22-23]: "But the fruit of the Spirit is love, joy, peace, longsuffering, gentleness, goodness, faith, meekness, temperance: against such there is no law."** This will form a basis and foundation, or "springboard" for all future studies, attainments, and accomplishments to follow in spiritual development and maturity. Indeed, this was the foundation upon which America was originally established and intended to continue to grow and develop from the strength and direction derived from these principles and their originator, Almighty Jehovah God Himself. This Spirit referred to here is the, Holy Spirit, the Spirit of the Most High God of the Bible. This "fruit" is a result of his divine nature of righteousness, holiness, purity, and unwavering absoluteness in his own devotion to his dedication and exercising of these eternally established principles.

There are other elements to this established set of Godly principles found elsewhere in the Bible, such as forgiveness, patience, compassion and others that need to be embraced, studied, learned and practiced. There are still others, such as, wisdom, the beginning of which comes with the reverencing of God, followed by, and including understanding, and knowledge. The lack of these causes destruction of all who reject this "knowledge of God" plus additional essential areas of knowledge supplied by God. **[Hosea 4:6].** There are other applications that can be made here. Then there is another quality, though not mentioned or recorded in God's word, of Godly "intelligence," the benefits of which would require its own presence and exercise. This is so closely associated with the requirement of "Godly wisdom," the difference, if there is any, may be hard to discern, however the wisdom and intelligence are needed for the proper, advantageous application of understanding and knowledge. There is another item that is an absolute necessity and companion of wisdom and intelligence that has pretty much dissipated into oblivion which used to benefit mankind considerably, but in our modern and post-modern times has been lost. That is good old fashioned **common sense.**

We have, unfortunately at the present time, a bunch of people who, having donned the black robes of the human courts, have rejected the white robes of God's righteousness, which begins with basic wisdom introduced by the fearing and reverencing of God. They are, with few exceptions, under their disguises of judges, some of our worst enemies of America today. These people, instead of defending, protecting, and advancing this Word of truth and deliverance individual and national; as judges were intended to do, are dedicated to making rulings against God's truth and absolutes, the truth that sets men and nations free from the abominations that are so prevalent where there is such a gross absence of God's word. Our present leadership is leaving a legacy of destruction for our children and we, for some reason have rejected or neglected the means to correct it, thus we also have to share in the blame. They have shown themselves opposed to the principles that have been the foundational structure of this nation and the all inclusive prosperity of her people.

I can only hope and pray that my writings will assist, at least a few, in the correction of the manifold transgressions man has heaped against God, His Christ, and His Word of righteousness. However, realizing humanity has had God's Word available at their fingertips for direction, correction, and counsel over many centuries past, *and the gross failure of mankind to adhere to it,* I have no misgivings about the success or failure or my writings to capture the attention of the multitudes. I do however, from the depths of my soul, thank God for leading of me into, and the glorious opportunity to present these writings under the unction, inspiration, and schooling of the Holy Spirit.

Man installed authorities and leaders cannot be rulers of people and nations; only this set of principles and the God who initiated them qualify to secure the well being of a people can be the ruler. Man, regardless of the amount of authority he claims, at his best can only be administrators and enforcers of these divine principles. Man without these God given principles operative within and among them is an utter failure and will bring that over which they bear rule to naught. Authorities and leaders are simply nothing more, nor nothing less than administrative authorities of these principles of God's righteousness. **[Luke 12:47-48]** They themselves, if they are to remain, and remain qualified as authorities and leaders, in whatever capacity they are awarded, must submit to these Godly principles or disqualify themselves and immediately be removed for the benefit of the nation and people. Those to whom men have committed much must now to be held accountable for their anti-American, anti-God, anti-society, subversive decisions and actions.

Those who are looking to other nations law's as guidelines to mold and make new laws for America should immediately be removed from office. America didn't become the greatest nation on earth by subscribing to the laws of other lesser nations in the past but by God's guidance in formulating her own laws based on Bible principles. These Bible principles were long standing before America was even thought of or imagined as a possibility in the minds of mortals, but were to become the foundational strength and stability of this great nation. If there is to be an adoption of other nation's laws, not based on Biblical influence and principle, for the guidance of another, let others adopt ours, which are based on those principles. I am afraid that we have strayed far from our calling as *"the land of the free and the home of the brave"*.

Those who propose lesser nations laws to be considered for America, are suspect as to their being either American or Christian, and certainly as qualified authorities and leaders, regardless of papers, positions, or titles held. **[1 Thessalonians 4:4]; "That every one of you should know how to possess his vessel in sanctification and honor."** This *"sanctification and honor"* is to be maintained according to God's standards and values, forming our attitudes and character which in the finality will identify us as Americans and Christians for the restoration of America's glory and honor. Papers of grand recognition, dispensing authority and noble titles will neither provide nor prove either one. Biblical orientated character, attitude, and lifestyle will prove what documents can only allude to, for **[Matthew 12:33], "the tree is known by his fruit."** The individual life, much less a nation, cannot be successfully managed outside of God's counsel, **[Psalms127: 1], "Except the Lord build the house; they labor in vain that build it".** Man cannot rule and reign over principles; principles must by necessity for the good of man, rule and reign over man and form his societies. Man at his best, can only be an administrator of such divine principles. These principles must proceed from an intelligence and capability that is exterior to and superior to man, yet be borne within his heart and mind, or he destroys himself and those he influences.

God is the only intelligence that meets this need of man and the universe which He himself created, and only he is qualified to manage it in its entirety with his own established set of principles. The stupidity of the idiot element of mankind seems to have no limits; and the only stupidity greater than that of those who exercise such idiocy and stupidity in their rule is manifested in those who allow them to continue to rule with such degraded character and blindly follow them, cheering them on without ever offering any opposition to them whatsoever.

Our nation did not become a sovereign nation and gain her independence, and greatness through the years of sacrifice, and dedication through the tens of thousand's of lives lost in their service, only to lose that sovereignty, greatness, and independence to the control of lesser men and nations opposed to the Biblical principles and foundation on which America has been established and built. Tolerance of stupidity, idiocy, and foolishness is intolerance of those things such as Godly wisdom, knowledge, understanding, intelligence, and the common sense needed to correct those conditions and situations that stupidity, idiocy, ignorance, and mans propensity for foolishness have created.

[James 4:4], "Ye adulterers and adulteresses; know ye not that the friendship of the world [of foolishness and stupidity] is enmity with God? Whosoever therefore will be a friend of the world is the enemy of God."

"Truth, crushed to earth will rise again; the eternal years of God are hers; while error, wounded, writhes in pain and dies among his worshippers." [William Cullen Byrant]

Christians are the bearers of this truth; they must now decide if they wish to resurrect their divine God ordained heritage, or perish with the nation they have neglected through their non-participation of national civil duties. America, you must reclaim the truth of God, which made you great, or die among those within you who embrace and practice error, rebellion, and abomination against God. Rest assured, if you tolerate sin in the camp, it will destroy you. It is time for the **[Job 4:21] "resurrection of the excellency that is in them"**, not only in the individual but in the nation by way of the individual. Without this "excellency" we die, even without wisdom, the wisdom that could have saved us. It is quite disturbing to watch our nation decline so rapidly as it has in the last several decades as man has increasingly turned his back on God and despised his word, **[Isaiah 5:24],** scorning the direction and correction that would deliver him from a multitude of the problems he has heaped upon himself.

Herein is another principle of truth in **[Hosea 4:7], "as they increased, so they sinned against me: therefore I will change their glory into shame."** America has seen great glory in her past: she has experienced a greatness that this world has never seen before nor ever will again unless God moves in a great and mighty way well beyond man's capabilities. This is dependent on mans repentance in obedience to God, **[2 Chronicles 7: 14], "If my people, which are called by my name, shall humble themselves, and pray, and seek my face, THEN will I hear from heaven, and will forgive their sin, and heal their land"**. This may, to a great extent, depend on our time spent in **[Hebrews 11:6],** exercising faith in God, believing that he is, and that he is a rewarder of those who diligently seek him. So far as his being a rewarder of those that diligently seek him; that is his business, but we can depend on him to honor his word.

There is no problem with God keeping his part of his covenant; the problem is on our part. Again in the **[James 4:7-10], "Submit yourselves therefore to God. Resist devil and he will flee from you."** The prerequisite to the devil fleeing from you is "submission to God." Too many are trying to resist the devil today and getting beat up for their efforts because they are neglecting the necessary "submission" relationship to God in order to have and enjoy their victories over the enemy. They cannot exist in their "if it feels good do it" culture and society and expect to experience that which God intends for them to have, life and life more abundantly through Jesus Christ our Lord and Saviour. Unfortunately we do not have a government that will even encourage its people to seek and serve the God that blessed us with this great nation we call home. This is something they could do without establishing a state church or religion if they had the courage, common sense, and intelligence to do it. The land of the free and the home of the brave is neither one if the courage to stand up for Jesus and proclaim his gospel of truth and absolutes is absent from the heart and mind; both being deceived by **the affection being set on the things on the earth, [Colossians 3:2].**

This way is being paved by demented leaders whose whole Christian experience consists of walking out of a church with a Bible under their arm for all to see. By their neglecting to "walk the walk", champion and encourage the Christian religion, they have, inadvertently, maybe intentionally, established a secular religion opposed to Biblical doctrine and counseling. In doing this, they have rendered illegal many things that would assist the spreading of the Christian doctrines of truth, the truth that if promoted and practiced would very possibly resurrect America's glory and dispel her present shame. It does seem that our present presiding judges are a major obstacle to that possibility, however. Let us pray that if they refuse to heed God's word that he will remove them by whatever means he may so choose and replace them with God-fearing men of dedication and obedience who are not afraid of the ACLU or any other Satan serving organizations or individual's. It certainly would seem that all the years of secular service and experience they have served in their different areas has led them to where they are now, and did not qualify them to lead in their respective positions of securing the nations well being, nor has it even served to enlighten them to the error of their ways.

As human beings, saved or otherwise, we do seem to have something in common; we learn slow: if at all, and very hard. How many devastating lumps does America have to take on her head, and how much ache in her heart to learn that she needs to repent and believe the gospel unto obedience? How deep into degradation must Americans sink before they realize that to change our ways, we must first change our thinking and thoughts, **[Isaiah 55:7-9].** All the secular teaching, training, and experience a person can accumulate over the years will never qualify them for the people skills needed for life without it all being established and anchored in the Biblical foundation of counsel and truth. What a horrible waste, to spend a life time pursuing and establishing secular careers without anchoring them in God's Word for the maximum eternal affect and benefit according to God's will. **[Matthew 16:26], "For what is a man profited, if he shall gain the whole world, and lose his own soul?"**

There is no doubt that God has ordained government, but he is working with quite a handicap, as all he has to work with are human beings with their frailties, sinful tendencies, impulses and pride that will not allow them to repent of their sin and stupidity. It would appear that this human experiment has been a colossal failure, but that maybe depends on whether you see the glass as half full or half empty. With many on the wide road that leads to destruction versus the few on the narrow way that leads to life everlasting, the glass is not half empty but neither is it half full. Regardless, it's how God sees it that counts, but [2 Peter 3:9], "the Lord is not **slack concerning his promise, as some men count slackness; but is longsuffering to us-ward, not willing that any should perish, but that all should come to repentance."**

Our opinions and thoughts about the situation don't really count as God has his own agenda and nothing man can think, say, or do will interrupt it. It would be well to our advantage, however as individuals, to explore God, his will and agenda and make sure we are prepared to be in total agreement with it and go along with it regardless of our position or place in life whether you are president, judge, ditch digger, or whatever, **[Acts10:34-35], "for God is no respecter of persons: But in every nation he that feareth him, and worketh righteousness is accepted, has favor, with him".** This would be a very intelligent and advantageous position to be in **"when the roll is called up yonder". Make sure you are there.**

NOTES

III.   WEIGHTIER MATTERS

[Matthew 23: 23-28], It seems as though in this grouping of scriptures there is a likeness to our national government as well as in some of the religious establishments. To often judgment, mercy, and faith along with other Godly traits and requirements, those unseen things of the spirit, heart and mind that are to **"accompany salvation", [Hebrews 6:9],** the things that constitute the "weighter matters" are rejected and, or simply neglected. This may be due to the fact they are never even thought of as characteristics that are essential to good living and life. They are intentionally omitted in favor of earthly, worldly concerns, attractions, and desires that cater to earthly demands based on feelings and emotions void of knowledge and uncontrolled by Godly wisdom and understanding. Here we find a graphic example of the "if it feels good do it culture" America has been drug into because of her ignorance, her lack of **"the knowledge of the Holy", [Proverbs 9: 10; Hosea 4:6].** This is in direct rebellion against God and his command and admonition to, **[Colossians 3:2], "Set your affection on things above, not on things on the earth".**

Not being of **"spiritually"** sound mind and body, man has a strong tendency, even in the church world, to set his affection on the "things on the earth". In the setting in the previous paragraph, **[Matthew 23: 23-28],** the scribes and Pharisee's were noted for paying tithes of mint, anise, and cumin, things of material value, things on the earth, while neglecting the "things above" of spiritual value such as **judgment, mercy, and faith, "the weightier matters of the law".** It would seem that this trait has remained with man down through the ages with the content of the bank account and pocketbook being considered above, and often in preference to the content and abundance of the heart which judgment, mercy, and faith and the other things of the divine nature which must be the priority for successful living and life. **"These things, being the essential priorities, ye ought to have emphasized and done, and not to leave the other undone"**.

To expand on this even further, we have the state imposed, ACLU enforced "Separation of Church and State" which, by shady constitutional law forbids the advancing of these Godly characteristics, **"the things above"** in public places simply because they are connected to Christian church "religious" teachings. This is primarily the reason and cause of America's demise and degradation she has been led into by her "leaders" and remains uncorrected by a lethargic population who cannot recognize destruction when it is staring them in the face; once again because of a **"lack of knowledge"**, and I'm beginning to realize, lack of concern.

God set the church in place for the explicit purpose of being the conduit for his gospel message of deliverance, redemption, and reconciliation to mankind for their temporal and eternal benefit. When man stepped in with his willful ignorance of the significance of this provision of God through Jesus Christ, this gospel message of deliverance from sin and iniquity, and intentionally plugged that conduit with his opposition of laws, rules, and regulations to that message, he robbed himself of all the benefits to be found within it. Only within the "weightier matters" of this message are found that which is essential to the well being and prosperity of humanity. Our illustrious Democratic Government with all its high profile shenanigans and maneuverings are rapidly taking the nation in the opposite direction with the help of many anti-God factions sympathetic to their cause; and all of these of **"our own countrymen"**.

However to the contrary, we find that religious input from non-Christian sources is being allowed, and encouraged by that allowance, in various places where Biblically taught and Christian practiced **"things above"** are forbidden, once again by constitutional and ACLU decree. There are additional organizations and individuals who are sympathetic to the erroneously imposed separation of church and state and ACLU views concerning Christianity. How the ACLU camel was allowed to get its nose in the tent for such devastating results to our nation and its people is quite interesting and happened over a long period of time through stealth and evil deception by our leaders and authorities, responsible for, but not **"keeping the heart of the nation [Biblical mandates] with all diligence"**, **[Proverbs 4: 23].** Now it issues forth death more than life. That's hard to dispute given the fact that, to date, some 50 million unborn babies have been slaughtered by the "legal" practice of abortion in this great democracy with the sexual promiscuity that causes it being consistently allowed, encouraged, and indulged in, even taught and promoted in some of our educational facilities. And your taxes are paying for it, Mr. and Mrs. America.

As certain of the Old Testament Kings "made their nation Israel to sin" because of their erroneous, inept leadership and abominations, so the same thing is happening today in our democratic America as has been occurring down through the ages under corrupt, evil leadership and governments. **[Ecclesiastes 1: 9], "The thing that hath been, it is that which shall be; and that which is done is that which shall be done: and there is no new thing under the sun".** Man's stupidity and ignorance is doomed to repeat itself over and over again: different time, different place, same song. That is pretty sick for a creation of creatures that sees themselves as intelligent beings. That intelligence was, however, Gods original intent. But it didn't take man long to mess it up and it has been messed up every since and is getting worse as there are more people with increasing ignorance to enlarge the mess.

[Hosea 4: 6-7], "As they increased, so they sinned against me, therefore will I change their glory into shame".

Thus does mankind in his **"lack of knowledge, wisdom, understanding, intelligence, and common sense", the Biblical given and taught principles of life versus death,** continue to wallow in the pit of his own abomination and filth of sin unto his self imposed destruction and it goes on century after century as **"no new thing under the sun",** then blames God, who he says he doesn't believe in, for his problems. Even with the multitudes of lives sacrificed to this stupidity, man refuses to learn anything. Thank God for the exceptions which have broken out of the mold with some intelligent choices to submit themselves to God for his counsel, correction, and direction, and the ultimate deliverance from sin, iniquity, and death, unto life and life more abundantly.

All this goes without even mentioning the multitude of other destructive practices, legal and illegal, that are so prevalent in our American society today that has ruined countless lives, psychologically, spiritually, financially and physically. **All this caused because of casting away, rejecting, despising, and neglecting the "weightier matters" that condition the heart and mind to the prosperity of the soul. Well has our old friend William Shakespeare said, "What fools ye mortals be"!** It certainly seems that humanity has worked over time to prove William's observation. It is difficult; maybe even impossible to view mans inhumanity to man with all his chaos, calamity, misery, murder, and mayhem he is heaping on himself without coming to that same conclusion. Thank God for the few exceptions of **[Matthew 7: 14], "who do find the strait gate and walk the narrow new and living way that leads to life".** They may be many, but are few in comparison to the multitudes which have rejected and neglected the "weightier matters of God's requirements".

[Deuteronomy 10: 12], "And now Israel [America, your name], what does the Lord thy God *REQUIRE* of thee, but to fear the Lord thy God, to walk in all his ways, and to love him, and to serve the Lord thy God with all thy heart and with all thy soul, To keep the commandments [Word] of the Lord, and his statutes, which I commanded this day or thy good. Just in case some of you missed it, **to walk in his ways** begins by thinking the way God thinks and having thoughts like his thoughts, **[Isaiah 55: 7-8].** That will involve a considerable amount of intense study, and will contribute to a better grasp and understanding of what these "weightier matters" consist of and why they are of such a necessity to each of us. *Though judgment, mercy, and faith are the only three listed here, they serve as examples of many others that are included in God's divine nature.*

[Matthew 23: 23] only gives us a brief example of these weightier matters and leaves it up to us to dig out and identify a multitude of others that wait to be discovered in our studies and research. Whether you like it or not, grace does not void out God's requirements of these things. Obedience is still a basic requirement beginning with **[Mark 1: 15], "Repent ye, and believe the gospel".** To really believe the gospel, we are going to have to find out what is in it. This takes some considerable time, study, and meditation. We spend a few short years in our secular schools to learn a few important things concerning how to dig out an existence in this world where we will spend a few short years attempting to develop, maintain and enrich that existence, but learn nothing about life unless someone is able to get through our thick heads of pride and ignorance to introduce us to Jesus Christ as Lord and Saviour and His Word of Life.

It is now we find that our real education begins after graduation from the worldly institutions of education when we have to make our own choices and decisions. If we make intelligent choices, we pass from an existence unto a life in

Christ; if we make erroneous choices, regardless of the extent of secular education, and possibly because of it, we remain in a condition of existence, howbeit for some that existence can be quite sumptuous, while for others of lesser means it becomes a day to day survival. Now as we attempt to apply the important things we have learned, we suddenly realize that there are some essential matters that need to be addressed that were neglected by educational authoritative decree. Unfortunately they were forbidden in our post modern schools by our so called leaders. Instead they substituted some trash courses that only intensified the problems. It is no wonder our educational system has gone to pot. No pun was particularly intended, but it is nevertheless part of the problem. Consequently the "weightier matters" of life were neglected, and the problems that have surfaced as a result of that are of a far more serious nature than simply having a flat tire on your car and finding out your spare is also flat.

Now we run into a problem within Christendom concerning some of the prevailing theology going around. If we see this as a command, it may be considered as a law, and if we are as saved by grace as some consider themselves to be, then we don't have to be concerned about obedience to God's Word because we are under grace and not under law. This in itself would constitute considerable ignorance, disobedience, and rebellion against God's requirements for righteousness and holiness.

Now the question has to be asked; how much of this disobedience is this wonderful gift of grace expected to cover, if any. It is true that we are saved by grace, but is it possible by accepting Jesus as personal Saviour and Lord, that we are obligated by a Biblical taught and inspired love for God to be willingly obedient to his desires and pleasure of holiness and righteousness without which no man will see God? **Maybe, just maybe, obedience itself is one of these "weightier**

matters" of the law that cannot be omitted simply because we are not under law, but under grace. It makes me wonder if these "weightier matters" have any comparison to the "higher powers" of **[Romans 13: 1]** that every soul is required to be subject to for the purpose of introducing and maintaining the unity among man and his God that Jesus is praying for in **[John 17].** It is just a thought that is worthy of consideration concerning **God's mandate to "do always those things that please him" [John 8: 29], by embracing and living "those things that accompany salvation" [Hebrews 6: 9].** There is indeed much to consider, if a person has a desire **to pass from darkness unto light, from death unto life, [John 5: 24], [Acts 26:18; Romans 13: 12].**

There is a multitude of legitimate material things on the earth that are essential to our livelihood and well-being which are all a part of God's vast, more than enough, provision and abundance. It is into this area, **[Psalms 24: 1; 50: 12; 89: 11]; [Haggai 2: 8]; [1 Corinthians 10: 26];** that the secular humanist, the atheist, etc, etc; all the non-believing elements of this world system who not only oppose God, but also themselves, have slithered by sleight of men and cunning craftiness. They have been for decades attempting to push the Christian out to clear a place for themselves for occupation in the hearts and minds of the population. This is an area that the Christian must repopulate by obedience in exercising boldness in proclaiming, declaring and re-establishing the Gospel of Truth.

If a person doesn't know enough about this gospel to declare and proclaim it, it is questionable if he even knows what he is defending. **[2 Corinthians 10: 4-6], "For the weapons of our warfare are not carnal, but mighty through God to the pulling down of strongholds; Casting down imaginations, and every high thing that exalteth itself against the knowledge of God, and bringing into captivity every**

thought to the obedience of Christ; And having a readiness to revenge all disobedience when your obedience is fulfilled". I question whether or not Christendom has a good working knowledge of what these weapons even consist of, or how to affectively use them. In a world of relativity, tolerance, acceptance , unlimited rights, diversity, if it feels good do it culture, etc, etc, it seems that these weapons have become irrelevant. **BUT GOD: his agenda is still right on target!**

For much to long the Christian has been preoccupied with "defending" this gospel instead of declaring and proclaiming it, not understanding that the truth, when established, will defend itself. **[John 15: 3], "Now ye are clean through the *[established, applied]* word that I have spoken unto you".** God has spoken it, inspired it, and confirmed it throughout the centuries past; it is up to us today to declare, proclaim, and establish it, in the hearts and minds of man in our time. **We "must be about our Fathers business", [Luke 2: 49].** We as Christians must see the absolute necessity of **[Colossians 3: 2], "Setting our affection on things above, not on the things of earth". "Truth crushed to the earth will rise again, the eternal years of God are hers; But error wounded, writhes in pain and dies among its worshippers", author; William Cullen Bryant.**

It is our, out of control, desire to acquire more than we need of these "things of earth" for whatever reason, usually selfishness, that man has used many excuses and questionable reasons to justify this, and has given us so many problems. Much of this has been used and abused due to plain old fashioned greed which has been a dominate human trait that is as old as sin itself, as well as a large part of it. However, much of God's abundance has been used to benefit man, but some of that usage even of questionable value in the progressive results. The biggest problems lay not necessarily in the things themselves, but the erroneous ways man has used them. To counter this we need to get a "new vision of the value "of the things above, such as wisdom, understanding, knowledge, Godly intelligence, and plain common sense and learn how and to put them to use. I am still learning these things, but I assure you, my allotted time on this earth will fail me, but these things given from God will never fail. **Proverbs 8: 10-12], verse 12, "I wisdom dwell with prudence, and find out knowledge of witty inventions".**

Certainly America has benefited from a multitude of "witty inventions" that have contributed greatly to her development and progress. Some of these "witty inventions" in being misused and abused have caused no end of problems in our land as well as other nations. They seemed like a good idea at the time, being developed by well intentioned men, but in the final analysis it seems all they have accomplished was some sort of erroneous, "population control". Man has learned nothing of profitable value through their invention and use of these questionable items. Wars have been won by use of them, but they have failed miserably to contribute to and bring a lasting peace. This can only be done by the **[Romans 12: 2], "renewing of the mind"** for the purpose for which it is to be renewed, to align our thoughts, thinking, and ways with Gods counsel and principles of life as revealed in His Word; **[Isaiah 55: 7-9], "Let the wicked forsake his way, and the unrighteous man his thoughts, and let him return to the Lord, and he will have mercy on him; and to our God, for he will abundantly pardon. For my thoughts are not your thoughts, neither are my ways your ways, saith the Lord. For as the heavens are higher the earth: so are my ways higher than your ways, and my thoughts than your thoughts".**

"Inventions" is an interesting word, though found only 5 times in the Bible, and 4 out of the 5 have to do with evil inventions devised in the heart of man. **[Romans 1:30]** speaks of these as being **"inventors of evil things"** and are included in with a whole list of others who indulge themselves in such things, verse 32, **"Who knowing the judgment of God, that they which commit such things *are worthy of death*, not only do the same, but have pleasure in them that do them"**. Maybe this is where the old saying "birds of feather flock together" came from; at any rate it's an interesting thought and seems to have merit. **[1 Corinthians 15:33], "Be not deceived, evil communications, companions, associations, etc, corrupt good manners and lifestyles"**. **[Proverbs 4:23], "Keep thy heart with all diligence; for out of it are the issues of life"**. The use of wisdom, knowledge, and understanding is in emphasis here. These are some additional things to be added to the list of "weightier matters". There are a great many of them that will surface as one gets more involved in searching the scriptures. Study them, learn them, apply them, **[Psalms 1: 2-3],** and may God's blessings be yours in your efforts and diligence.

NOTES

____

____

____

____

____

____

____

____

____

IV.   STATE OF THE HEART

There are many scriptures that pertain to the conditioning, or the "State of the Heart." We are instructed in **[Proverbs 4: 23],"Keep thy heart with all diligence; for out of it are the issues of life."** It would seem that the need for "diligence" is emphasized here simply by the use of the word. No half hearted attempt at developing and maintaining of character and abundance of heart is acceptable. It will always be insufficient to the need and will invariably fall short of the requirements needed for the heart to issue forth life rather than death. Of such is the nature of man unless there is something exterior to his natural inclination of sinfulness that is able to correct and direct his life's journey. Several scriptures in The Psalms point to the relationship with God as involving the "whole heart" in various ways. I would encourage the readers to search these scriptures out for in-depth study for benefit of knowledge that can be passed on to others and for the benefit of all. Therein do we find the admonition to **"hide God's word in our heart so that we might not sin against him"**, [Psalms 119: 11].

Now we have to bring the mind into consideration as the heart and mind are quite often linked together and may mean the same thing as all inclusive of the new man. We find this in **[Romans 12: 2]** where the heart is not mentioned but the necessity of a "diligently" kept, prepared, and renewed mind is of the utmost importance, **"Be not conformed to this world, but be ye transformed by the "diligent" and continual renewing of your mind, that ye may prove what is that good, and acceptable, and perfect will of God."** It would seem that if there is going to be a proving in our lives of what is that good, and acceptable, and perfect will of God, it can only take place through the avenue of a "diligently kept heart and renewed mind." This is all based on the input of God's word of truth and absolutes for daily counsel and guidance that has been **"hid, stored, in the heart and becomes the "abundance of**

64

the heart" [Luke 6: 45]. You may well be a recipient of God's amazing grace, but if you neglect the requirements that produce a renewed mind and diligently kept heart, you will lead a defeated, problematic life, even as a professing Christian. The evil output of an evil heart mentioned in this scripture emphasizes the need for the heart and mind to be in the constant care and nurturing of God's Word. This, of course is based on our own choice. **"Therefore choose life that both thou and thy seed, descendents, children, may live", [Deuteronomy 30:19].** There is one of two things which may work together simultaneously that are needed here for this choice to be made. First, there is the intelligence to perceive the "goodness of God" and choose it for its own value and resultant benefits and rewards, or the desperation to escape the sinful existence and problems that accompany and are characteristic of this sin orientated existence.

Several years ago there was a catchy little phrase that was used quite extensively by many who wished to show some semblance of brilliance and glean some admiration and esteem from others by the use thereof. That phrase was *"state of the art"*, which as I understand, was meant to convey a thought of extreme quality to the object being referred to. It was quite an impressive little quote and sounded equally impressive to the benefit of those who used it, and I suppose many of those who heard it being used. Although it never made much sense, at least it sounded good and seemed to convey the thought as was intended. It was used in a different sense with a different meaning as the president would give his state [condition] of the union, or nation, address, a pastor his state of the church address, or others their state of whatever they were speaking of address. If it was a large corporation, such as Enron, the state, or condition maybe was not as it was presented to be and consequently people suffered great loss. But such is the result of deception for whatever purpose the deceiver has in mind. But like all fads, the "state of the art" usage seemed to have run its course, lost its punch and prestige, and is seldom heard anymore.

However, regardless of the state, or condition of what was being referred to, it seems to be the nature of man to be a little bit fraudulent in his presentation of that state, especially if there were hidden agendas and discrepancies afoot; which if they were planned discrepancies, reveals the "state of the heart", or possibly "hearts", of those in control of such events. It is this condition, the "state of the heart" that I wish to call attention to in this writing. This as a condition that the Bible addresses from cover to cover, a condition we all have to deal with on a moment by moment, daily basis that produces temporal benefits that must be properly viewed and experienced to be appreciated as well as eternal benefits and rewards promised, but yet to be enjoyed. The basic difference between the Biblical "state of the heart" versus a non-biblical condition is found in several scriptures, a notable one in **[Deuteronomy 30:19]**, mentioned previously. The Biblical conditioned state of the heart is rewarded with life and blessing, whereas the non-biblical condition of evil and abomination is cursed with death and additional cursing. I make no claim to being the smartest person in the world, but even I can figure out that life and blessing with their eternally extended benefits and rewards are much to be desired and preferred to death and cursing with their resultant daily and eternal penalties.

The majority of stuff this catchy little ditty was applied to was just that, "stuff", of material content, the value of which seldom, with exceptions, lasted as long as the ditty did and was seldom as impressive as the ditty sounded. There are other things that have come on the scene of humanity that I would have to regard as truly "state of the art" quality. There are things that have come, remained, and blessed mankind; some in their existence, but others in their usage as their existence continues. Even the existence of the Bible, regardless of its value, which will always remain, becomes negligible in its benefits if it is not put to its intended use. Writings of glorious nature, that have come at the inspiration of divine guidance that have touched the hearts and minds of concerned individuals, have truly brought life and life more abundantly to those who "gladly received" such words. These words of instruction and knowledge are at the height, and above man perceived, the "state of the art" quality, as they are instrumental in securing the God required "State of the Heart" that is essential for this life and life more abundantly. Man has settled for a multitude of stuff that has been considered as "state of the art", stuff that has robbed him of more than it could possibly contribute to his good and wellbeing; stuff that was never designed for his benefit, but only for gratification of his feelings and emotions and make the producers of such items wealthy.

There are other things that must be considered such as the art of paintings that have commended themselves to the list of notables, and some music compositions that provide stirrings to the soul and revitalization to the spirit that have remained of great aesthetic and spiritual value to humanity long after the composers of such paintings and music have passed on. There is much to be considered here as to the "state of the heart" of these various artists with their contributions to mankind along with what inspired and compelled them to produce such stirring items. Regardless, somewhere along the way we must realize that such contributions of the various talents could not be accomplished without God's contribution of his likeness and excellence within us that enabled such conditions, items, and events.

There are people who would seem to be handicapped who do some rather astounding things, such as playing a piano. Where did such talent come from when not learned by conventional means? Why do some people have natural abilities to do certain things and excel at them while others do not? Some people can do by natural abilities what others have to learn, sometimes with great difficulty, from "scratch", and even then never seem to arrive to where the "naturalists" excelled with a minimum of effort. Much is to be learned and acknowledged of God's greatness and majesty with which he has so generously and abundantly blessed humanity. And all he asks of us is to honor him with obedience to his divine principles, **[Matthew 22: 37-40], "Jesus said unto him, Thou shalt love the Lord thy God with all thy heart, and with all thy soul, and with all thy mind. This is the first and great commandment. And the second is like unto it, Thou shalt love thy neighbor as thyself. On these two commandments hang all the law and the prophets."**

If man would exercise himself to know, understand, and meet the demands of this "love", what a different world we would have today. Regardless of the abundance of grace, there are certain conditions and demands that are necessary for meeting the requirements of this love. These things are all basically contained in being willingly "obedient".

There is an abundance of knowledge man needs to attain to, **[Hosea 4:6], as requirements for life, living, health, peace, and happiness;** and at the head of this list of requirements would have to be, of course, THE HOLY BIBLE with it's introduction of Jesus Christ, Saviour and King to humanity; God's own Living Word to mankind for his guidance, nurture, prosperity, and profit, which man generally, has to his own demise, rejected, and despised. Well has William Shakespeare said **"What fools ye mortals be"!** Unfortunately, even in some Christian circles this Word is neglected to the point of creating some "gates of hell" within the body of Christ and erecting some strongholds that are a constant source of irritation, thorns in the flesh, or worse, so to speak. It is a part of God's goodness, **[Romans 2: 4],** that God's grace "is sufficient" for our spiritual maintenance whenever we stumble and fall along the way. But his counsel and direction is not only sufficient, but absolutely essential for our Spiritual growth and development unto the smashing of these gates of hell and pulling down strongholds unto victory, not settling for mere maintenance while tolerating these oppositions to the gospel. It is and has always been God's intention that we be **[Romans 8:37] "more than conquerors through him that loved, and continues to love, us"**.

To read these words of divine counsel, to acknowledge, accept them, and claim to believe them and yet not to put forth executive effort to attain to their intended purpose is to insult God and our Lord Jesus Christ, the cleansing power of his blood and his name. **[Romans 6: 19; 22], "I speak after the manner of men because of the infirmity of your flesh: for as ye have yielded your members servants to uncleanness and to iniquity unto iniquity; even so now**, at least to the extent you served sin, **yield your members servants to righteousness unto holiness". Verse 22: "But now being made free from sin, and become servants of God, ye have your fruit unto holiness, and to the end everlasting life"**. Therefore, **[Matthew 6: 33], "Seek ye first the kingdom of God *and his righteousness;* and all these things, verse 32 that ye have need of, shall be added unto you"**.

Does this include "Restoring America,", or "Reviving Oregon's Amazing Roots" as there certainly seems to be a need for this? There is no doubt, a renewed long lost zeal in proclaiming the gospel in the face of the opposition of "our own countrymen" would be a good place to put our energies. There are many scriptures that express this as God's commands and will, and certainly is among **"doing those things that always please Him, [John 8: 29], and the better things that accompany salvation", [Hebrews 6:9].** This would contribute significantly to the "state of the hearts" and minds as well as our overall living standards. Who knows, we might even learn how to **[1 Peter 1:22], "Purify our souls in obeying the truth through the Spirit unto unfeigned love of the brethren and to love one another with a pure heart fervently"**. My goodness, what a change and enrichment of life this would be.

In **[Genesis 1:26]** we find that God made man in his own image and likeness which included a Godlike "State of the Heart" that can be reclaimed today thru God's provision of Jesus Christ as Lord and Saviour, redeeming us and reconciling us back to God for the purpose of restoring this "State of the Heart" condition to us. This Godlike "state of the heart", condition is commensurate with the **"excellence that is in them that goes away" found in [Job 4:21].** Without this **"excellency"**, being diligently exercised, it dissipates and **"goes away, and they die "even without wisdom"**. Enter here, the *"use it or lose it"* concept, the **"exercising of oneself to Godliness, [1 Timothy 4: 7].** Though saved and born again through the blood of Jesus, this condition of God's likeness and excellency, the "State of the Heart", does not necessarily return as an automatic result of accepting Jesus. This does requires the challenge of **[2 Timothy 2: 15], "Studying to show thyself approved unto God, a workman that needeth not to be ashamed, rightly dividing the word of truth" and [Acts 10:35], "fearing, or reverencing of God and working of righteousness".** All of this is in relationship **to loving God with all you heart, soul mind, might, etc, and [Matthew 6:33] "seeking first the [establishing and operation] of the kingdom of God, and his righteousness"** within you for the required **state of the heart. This is a heart that is kept with all Biblical diligence out of which comes the issues of life, [Proverbs 4:23].** This all is required along with, and is a significant part of **"being saved by grace"**.

God gives us some real insight into the result of man's abdication of his **[Genesis 1:26]** God given dominion authority over the works of his hands, **[Psalms 8: 3-9].** It can be accurately referred to as Satan usurping the God given power and authority of man through his masterful deception, **"for Satan is a liar and the father of lies", [John 8: 44].** To a large extent this is correct, but then as now, it can only happen if man abdicates this authority, which those who are rebellious and disobedient have already done by such rebellion and disobedience. Jesus paid the redeeming price, not only for man's transgression but also for the returning of his creation back into the control of the **"glorious liberty of the children of God", [Romans 8: 19-23].** Obviously this portion of scripture has future reference to it, but when we finally develop to the point where **"sin has no more dominion over us", [Romans 6: 14],** surely this will be of great benefit to our land as well, to be applied today.

But we will wait in hope of God's fulfilling his agenda for earth as we haven't done to good with the agenda God delivered to us to perform. The "State of the Heart" of the Christian family, in a general sense, has not faired to well. There were however, individuals who were able to provide enough spiritual stability to keep the church going in its general intended direction. There were, and unfortunately still are, however, some "gates of hell" established thru disunity, which is one of the most deceitful gates, along with disobedience and rebellion on an individual level, among and within the various denominations. These "gates" have hindered to a great extent the absolute spiritual development and advancement of the church. This was the result of man attempting to build the church without adequate submission to God and his counsel. **[Psalms 127: 1], "Except the Lord build the house, they labor in vain that build it".** Consequently, today we have "churches" that have embraced thoughts and ways totally contrary to Biblical directives for righteousness, holiness, and spiritual virtue. Jesus witnessed this and announced in **[Matthew 16:18] "that he was going to build his own church**

against which these man made gates of hell could not prevail".

The state of the heart outside the Christian family, due to its ever increasing evil abundance, has been, and continues to be, absolutely disastrous, and our beloved nation and her people are paying a horrible price for such idiocy. **[Hosea 4: 7], "As they were increased, so they sinned against me: therefore will I change their glory into shame".** America is experiencing this shamefulness today she has brought on herself, not at the hands of foreign powers, but at the internal rejection of God and his power to save and deliver, **[2 Chronicles 7: 14],** victimizing herself by her own self imposed ignorance and stupidity. Though the principle was recorded thousands of years ago, it still bears its truthful, bitter fruit, **[Hosea 4: 6], "My people are destroyed for lack of knowledge: because thou hast rejected knowledge, I will also reject thee that thou shalt be no priest to me: seeing thou hast forgotten the law of thy God, I will also forget thy children".** This principle, though primarily and originally given to the Israelites, applies to all men everywhere for all time. It is, as the rest of God's Word is, still in force; no part of it can ever be rescinded, and it supersedes anything and everything man can bring in opposition against it including the "supreme" court with it's erroneous, contemptible efforts to rule and reign in God's stead through their feeble but "legal" attempts to **"form weapons against it's truth and absolutes",** **[Isaiah 54:17], [Psalms 1: 4-6; 2].** This certainly includes their imposition of the "separation of church and state" which has crippled the church's effectiveness to the people and sealed the fate of the state by excommunicating God and his word from the public square, including our institutions of education at all levels. Indeed **"what fools ye mortals be".**

Though a proper state of the heart is important to all, it is especially essential for leaders, as they are the ones who must serve as examples to teach and condition those who come after them that will eventually fill their positions of leadership. When I refer to a "proper state of the heart" I must emphasize that which is founded exterior to man's evil nature which tends to his own demise. There is only one source where this proper life giving instruction, counsel, and strength can be found, and that is in Almighty God through Jesus Christ. God and God alone has what man needs to live and move and have his being according to God's own design for growth, development, and overall prosperity for, not only man, but for God's entire creation. The world and certainly America is manifest proof of this through man's excommunication of God, and is evidenced by the decrepit condition of humanity and the world they have polluted by means of their sin and abominations. Thank God for the "few" exceptions, **[Matthew 7:14; Luke 13:24],** who have been true to their calling and have maintained the truth, counsel, and direction of God's Word. **These, by God's grace, have sustained and enriched the brightness of their light and the savor of their saltiness.** They have shown the way and preserved many within God's care.

Unfortunately America has many "leaders" in various places of influence who have chosen **death and cursing, [Deuteronomy 30:19] rather than life and blessing,** and are continually in the process of contaminating the nation with their foolish choices in opposition to God and his truth. They are somewhat reminiscent of the three classes of persons found in **[Matthew 23], scribes, Pharisee's, and hypocrites,** who neither enter into God's kingdom and go to great lengths to prevent others from going in as well, **vs., 13**. All this anti-Bible, anti-God, anti-Christian religion being imposed by pseudo authorities is robbing the American public of the wisdom, knowledge, and understanding that is needed to prevent eventual destruction, which as we can see in America today, is well on its way. It doesn't take much intelligence to see our beloved America today is in more of a condition of digression than it is progression, especially in a correct spiritual sense, which in reality forms the foundation for everything else.

If America is to be restored to her former glory, it is essential to realize it will only occur on the foundation of a people who have set themselves in obedience to God to resurrect the excellency that was originally created within them. This must be done, not to restore America, but primarily to bring glory, honour, and pleasure to God, which is the only condition on which America could be restored. The restoring of "spiritual" America must precede any attempt to reclaim our heritage, for our heritage consists of, and is founded on a Biblical spiritual heritage. Deny this, as is being done in our courts, and we bring destruction on ourselves, for to deny this is to choose death and cursing, **[Deuteronomy 30:19-20].**

NOTES

V.   MIND MALFUNCTION

It is amazing how much we hear and see about obesity, eating wrong foods, eating the right foods or to much of either one, drinking high calorie drinks etc. etc; So much about the body condition, the abbs, exercise, injecting of harmful substances, steroids, taking the right vitamins' dieting, etc, etc, and on and on it goes. No one ever seems to consider the brain, the mind, often referred to in the Bible as "the heart" or the "inner man", our mental computer center, yet there is every bit as much, and maybe more, junk and trash poured and crammed into it as there is harmful garbage into the body, and in addition, it is much, much, more deadly. It is, after all the condition of the mind that opens the door for all the entrance of everything else, whether it be good or evil, righteous or unrighteous.

Just like body junk, American's have an insatiable appetite for psychological junk food and have proven themselves to be every bit as gluttonous in this area as they are in other areas. There is a thing the computer people have; GIGO, or garbage IN, garbage OUT. That is not quite accurate so far as our mental computers are concerned, for in these "psychological" computers garbage comes in, is stored and grows, and grows and ferments, is mixed with additional mind destructive garbage and grows some more, being sent out in ever increasing blobs of repulsive filth and degradation or in clever deceptions that appear somewhat desirous to lure the unsuspecting victim. In the natural state, without this evil somewhat judicially protected trash; this being, properly conditioned and taught, this unsuspecting victim would be turned off by this repulsive filth and degradation. However, the subtlety of it is somewhat reminiscent of the great deception, packaged as desirable, in the Garden of Eden; try it, you'll like it, *"ye shalt not surely die"*, and the lie continues to destroy the multitudes, packaged, promoted, in many instances legalized and glamorized by the anti-God, anti-Bible, anti-Christ elements within our own nation of *"our own countrymen"*. These traitors of humanity are found from the gutters to the highest authorities and positions mankind has held in our governmental areas, as well as all other areas.

There is hardly a day goes by without an official of some capacity being brought down by some erroneous practice they have indulged in for whatever reason or excuse. We have not as yet even addressed the subject of mind-altering drugs that people steal and kill to get their hands on to satisfy their own lust of self-gratification. On the one hand we have the minds that are terribly obese with destructive physiological fat with input from trash television shows and such like including pornography etc., perverting the mind where it couldn't think a decent thought if it were paid to do so because it has not been trained and conditioned to do so. On the other hand we have the minds; they are often the same ones, which are starving for lack of intelligent growth and development which is virtually non-existent anymore in our humanist, secularist, world that has excommunicated God.

[Ecclesiastes 12:12] gives us a good insight into this lack of intelligent growth and development as to the reason for such lack; **"much study is a weariness to the flesh"**. There are many and various reasons why minds are in a state of intelligence malnutrition and thus malfunction, and plain old laziness seems to be one of the most prevalent ones. Another reason that is not recognized by our "officials" is the subtle leading away from areas of intelligence and sound Godly reasoning. This has come about in our modern society where the everyday demands of life, some justified and some not, have put a burden of "busy-ness" on people, and robbed them of the time, effort, and diligence needed to **[Psalms 1: 2]**,

"delight in, meditate on, and study of God's Word to glean from it the essential knowledge that would avert their destruction", [2 Timothy 2: 15; Hosea 4:6].

Regardless of the multitude of different contributing factors, they have all had their devastating effects in putting distracted and lazy minds in a state of constant malfunction. This is a consistent world condition with man struggling in his pride and stupidity to do things his own way regardless of God's direction and counsel. This world is not in the degraded shape it is in by God's design and intelligence, but by mans rebellion, rejection, and disobedience of God and his word. These three things in their relationship to God; rebellion, rejection, and disobedience can best be summed up in two words: gross stupidity, or one word "sin". In light of the present and eternal blessings that are available through a born-again relationship with God through Jesus Christ, it can only be spiritual blindness born of "Mind Malfunction" that causes such stupidity.

Really, where has all the intelligence that God originally designed into mans being gone to? As the body heals after it is wounded, so the earth has its own healing qualities, rebounding after mans desecration of it; but the mind, that gray matter computer located in the attic of your house of clay that you are living in is a different situation. Wound it, desecrate it, damage it, and you may well be done for the rest of your life. Yet man does this to himself, to each other, and still claims to be an intelligent being. It is all based on, and continued because man suffers from a terminal condition. I refer to this as B.A.D.D., and indeed it is, BIBLE ATTENTION DEFICIT DISORDER, resulting in acute cases of MIND MALFUNCTION that is a world wide epidemic, the effect of it being felt by all, even those who have not contracted it. It is worse than it sounds. It alone has destroyed more nations and people, brought down more empires, wasted more time, effort, energy, cost more lives and fortunes than any other thing mankind has ever experienced throughout all history. It may well be termed as the ultimate WMD, and we all harbor its potential in our minds. It alone has and is responsible for, and has caused every lesser disease known plus the dilemma's man experiences every day of his life. More people have been destroyed by this than from any disease known to man, and yet mankind revel's in it, suffers from it, is made destitute by it, dies from it, and still claims to be free.

Those affected with acute cases of B.A.D.D., remind me of those described in **[Matthew 23:27], "for ye are like unto whited sepulchers, which indeed appear beautiful outward, but are within full of dead men's bones"**. The one big exception being that many of them don't appear very beautiful any more. Again I must recall a Shakespeare quote: **"What fools ye mortals be"**. **[Isaiah 26: 7-10] 7, "The way of the just is uprightness: thou, most upright, dost weigh the path of the just. Vs. 8, In the way of thy judgments, O LORD, have we waited for thee; the desire of our soul is to thy name, and to the remembrance of thee. Vs. 9, With my soul have I desired thee in the night; yea, with my spirit within me will I seek thee early;** *for when* **THY JUDGMENTS are in the earth, the inhabitants of the world will learn righteousness, [and not until then]. Vs.10, Let favour be shown to the wicked, yet he will not learn righteousness; in the land of uprightness will he deal unjustly, and will not behold the majesty of the Lord"**. If your mentality is not free from sin and its devastating results, you are a slave to it even though you may enjoy its involvement while at the same time being disgusted with it, and you cannot escape from its eventual destruction on your own. You need God's assistance and help as we all have and still do.

There is no such thing, where sin is concerned, as simply turning over a new leaf or making a new years resolution. **[John 3:3-8]** **"Ye must be born again**, vs.6, **That which is**

born of the flesh is flesh; and that which is born if the Spirit is Spirit". You cannot change the fact that your fleshly body is caught in an aging process and is deteriorating. But your Spirit, your Soul, the real eternal you that resides within it, being in an intimate relationship with God through accepting of Jesus Christ as Lord and Saviour, the **"born again of water and of the Spirit" by "repentance and believing the gospel"** has a positive effect on the condition of that **[Job 4:19]** house of clay you are living in at the present time. The deterioration and ultimate death of your "house of clay" is nothing in light of dying to sin by being born again unto life and life more abundantly through Jesus Christ. Personally, regardless of the fact that God has blessed me with good health, I am looking forward to a new glorified body that will never grow old. I'll trade this old one with its aging, grunts, groans, creaks, and failing abilities in exchange for the promised new one anytime.

In the light of God's abundant provision, **death has no sting and the grave has no victory, [1Corinthians 15:55-57].** I've had a good life and hope to enjoy a few more good years as long as I'm here, but I have no problems concerning the physical death that this body of flesh will experience by and by. I will depart this vessel of clay in which I now live; **it will return to the dust of the ground from whence it came, and I will return to the Lord from whence I came, [2 Corinthians 5:8]. [Philippians 1:21-24]. "For me to live is Christ, and to die is gain"**. Look around you, though there are some good things in this world to be enjoyed that were created by God for us to enjoy, however, man in his sin encroaching contamination, is making that peaceful enjoyment more difficult day by day. It is amazing; we get sick, catch a disease, go to the doctor for a cure, but the disease of the mentality, B.A.D.D., Bible Attention Deficit Disorder is accepted as a common condition without realizing it is a deadly disease affecting the mind, heart, soul, and body. **[Job 4:19-21] "They, that dwell in houses of clay, vs.19, are destroyed from**

morning to evening: they perish forever without any regarding it. Doth not their excellency which is in them go away? They die, even without wisdom".

People without Biblical knowledge are totally unaware of what is happening in their lives. **[Hosea 4:6], "My people, any people, are destroyed for lack of knowledge: because thou hast rejected knowledge, I will also reject thee, that thou shalt be no priest to me: seeing thou hast forgotten the law of thy God, I will also forget thy children".** This last part of this verse relating to our children being affected by our conduct is a bit of a sobering thought. It is understandable when you consider, as parents and adults, we pass our influence on to our children. If we are obedient unto the Lord and teach his values and principles of obedience to our children, they are likely to follow our instructions; if we do not, both, we, and God lose them, and we see it going on continually in our American society. Many, not all, young people are out of control, quite often because parents are out of God's control and as the old saying goes: the apple doesn't fall far from the tree. Thank God for his intervention that does cause some apples to fall far from the parent trees. Thank God for young minds that do get a hold of God, and as a result do not "malfunction".

The call, the challenge, the responsibility, is to the parents, beginning with you, DAD, as the head of the house, being the foundation, grounded and anchored in the word of God, his counsel, his instructions for the formation, direction, and strength of your family. Leaders; civic, secular, and spiritual, I couldn't care less what you erroneously claim as "separation of church and state", you have the same responsibility under God to care for the well-being of those you have jurisdiction over as a father does those under his care. If you do not have the courage to shoulder that responsibility, you should have the courage, honesty, and decency to remove yourself and make room for someone who does and will.

If you refuse to carry out your obligations and responsibilities to God and your constituents, then those constituents need to muster up the courage to unceremoniously, remove you, and replace you, post-haste. We all as Christians must be aware of this fact; and non-Christians, definitely including those in authoritative positions, made aware of the fact that regardless of all his struggles, wars fought, victories won, lives lost, heartaches endured, tears shed, fortunes made and wasted, etc. etc. etc., man cannot, will not, learn nor accomplish anything of real, lasting, value until he learns and implements God's righteousness and holiness to the establishment of his kingdom. Until then, all man's efforts, maneuverings, and manipulations are nothing but exercises of futility tuned to a worldly rejection and neglect of God and his Son Jesus Christ our Lord. **[Romans 12:3] "And be not conformed to this world, but be ye transformed by the renewing of your mind[s], that you may prove what is that good, acceptable, and perfect will of God".**

I do not intend to leave the impression that what man has accomplished in that which is to his overall benefit constitutes complete failure, but I would be remiss if I seemed to allow these accomplishments, as great and essential as they may be, to be equated to the absolute need to be born again into the presence of God experience through Jesus Christ our Saviour, Lord, and yes, **our soon coming King. [Revelation 22:11] "He that is unjust, let him be unjust still: and he which is filthy, let him be filthy still: and he that is righteous, let him be righteous still: and he that is holy, let him be holy still".** We, however, who have repented of our sin and have been made the righteousness and holiness of God through the cleansing power of the Blood of Jesus our Saviour, are going home. Praise God for his faithfulness, love, and forgiveness manifested through our Lord and Saviour Jesus Christ.

NOTES

VI.   THEY PERISH FOREVER

[Hosea 4:19-20] "They, who dwell in houses of clay, are destroyed from morning to evening: THEY PERISH FOREVER without any regarding it". In light of the hurricane Katrina disaster that befell the masses that were warned about the magnitude of the storm that was headed their way and did not regard those warnings; I could not help but think of this scripture in Hosea concerning the those who do not regard warnings of coming disasters, never considering that maybe it wasn't the disaster that destroyed them but the lack of regarding or heeding the warnings and taking the proper steps that would have avoided being destroyed. The warnings were given several days prior to the hurricane hitting the gulf coast, thus giving sufficient time to take evasive measures. Why were not the warnings REGARDED? Is it because people just plain don't like being told what to do and their built in pride naturally rejects submission to direction from others? There are many and varied reasons or excuses that could be given for not regarding warnings of coming disasters. How could those caught in such disasters after they had received ample warnings of the "wrath to come" have sufficient reason for disregarding the warnings and not even have a justifiable excuse for doing such disregarding?

We don't have that much information about the people who were witnesses to the building of Noah's ark or the purpose for which it was built. But due to man's nature, it is fair and quite accurate to assume that Noah and his family received considerable adverse publicity during the construction period; this is putting it mildly. Once again we have a graphic example of disregarding warnings about a major storm, the result of which makes Katrina quite insignificant by comparison. In spite of man's contrariness, opposition, and continued disregarding the warnings, Noah remained true to God's commandment and instructions in building the Ark However in **[Genesis 5: 5-13],** we find that God had already passed judgment on the people for their wickedness, evil, violence corruption etc. We can only guess as to how the catastrophes we see in our modern times are a result of the same conditions among the earth's populace, but God still gets the blame for it all. Amazing how we never hear about God getting credit and thanks for the good things, but is always blamed for the bad things; Oh, it's an act of God. We have been experiencing some beautiful days here in the Willamette Valley in Oregon and I enjoy thinking of them as "an act of God", his blessings to behold and enjoy, and giving Him much thanks for it.

People disregard the warnings of sexually transmitted diseases and "are destroyed from morning to evening" because of their disregarding the continued warnings. So the disaster in that area continues "without any regarding it". The drug activity is another area of continual destruction because many do not regard nor heed the warnings. There are many things in our American society and indeed the world where people are destroyed because they lack the intelligence to heed and "regard the warnings", which if regarded, could, and in most cases would avert disaster. We find a major warning in **[2 Chronicles 7: 14]** about the land being under siege and desperately in need of healing which will not take place until people regard the warnings, **"If my people, which are called by my name, shall *humble themselves, and pray, and seek my face, and turn from their wicked ways;* THEN will I hear from heaven, and will forgive their sin, and will heal their land"**. Repentance remains the requirement for disobedience with the four ingredients of repentance given in the above scripture.

In listening to discussions on television about the "aftermath" of the Katrina storm and seeing the destruction, I couldn't help but think about the warnings God has continually given humanity for centuries about the storm of sin and iniquity that has raged in the hearts and souls of men throughout the ages, and its aftermath; warnings that for the most part go disregarded and scoffed at, the aftermath of which will make Katrina look like a Sunday School picnic. And to add to those warnings, here I am re-emphasizing those warnings which will continue to be scoffed at and rejected; but that's not my problem regardless of my concern. We will have to leave that up to the scoffers and rejecters to face by themselves. They will have plenty of time, like an eternity, to regard and regret their idiocy of disregarding and rejection of the warnings "of the wrath to come". I will be much to busy enjoying heavens glories to think about them and feel sorry for them.

I do not intend to sound callous and unconcerned about the plight of the unsaved, it's just that I cannot do their regarding for them nor can I make their choices for them. I do, however, stand with **God as he is not willing that any should perish, but that all should come to repentance and believe the gospel, [2 Peter 3: 9].** God in his love and mercy has made provision for deliverance from a multitude of immediate problems and problems that lurk in the future to ambush those who refuse to avail themselves of God's provision of deliverance today. **This provision has a name and it is Jesus Christ. He has an appointment scheduled for you; don't miss it.** There is another appointment scheduled for you somewhere in your future that you cannot escape or dodge. In view of that appointment, I would sincerely urge and advise you to keep the first one to be delivered from the second one.

In the progression of confusion and chaos this world is experiencing today, calamity is certain tomorrow. That is not based on the way I feel, it is what God has been warning us about for centuries. Isn't his love, longsuffering and patience wonderful? We don't seem to have anywhere near the intelligence as God has love and patience. Maybe that's why we are told in the Bible that the "fear, or reverence, of the Lord is the beginning of wisdom, knowledge, and understanding", and just for good measure I'll include intelligence with those. I really don't believe the Lord will mind at all. It seems from this, that until we get to the point of revering God as God we are a pretty stupid bunch, for only then does wisdom begin to appear. Well anyhow it's something to think about, or regard, if you are inclined to think at all. This might be a new experience for you as thinking would be to many, but stretch your mind, it'll get used to it.

In the aftermath of Katrina there has been considerable discussion and announcements about the rebuilding of New Orleans. Much has been said about the poverty situation that existed there. There is an area that has not been discussed to the extent it needs to be to bring about a proper solution. Poverty of material goods and finances are important to address, but it is the poverty of mentality that is causing the problems. This is not restricted to the people who are out of work, have low paying jobs, or simply refuse to work for whatever excuse is used, it also applies to a vast number of others, many of whom are referred to and considered as leaders. That term, "leaders" must be applied loosely in many circumstances and situations as we have many leaders who definitely do not possess the requirements and Biblical qualifications to do what has to be done, thus it is not getting done.

How often have we heard that the solution to our problems is more education. This is true if the "more education" was "better education" that includes as a priority, the essentials of Christian character building This also depends entirely on whether or not those in need of such education will avail themselves of it. We have people who are well educated in the ways to work the welfare system for personal immediate benefits, but in the long run they destroy themselves and any others they influence and educate in their dubious skills. We have many people who are educated in many things that are contrary to common sense, intelligence, and whatever else is essential to the overall well being of themselves, our society, and nation. We have many of these in our political establishment, judicial areas, institutions of higher education, and about every other area where people are involved, which doesn't compliment humanity very well.

Several years ago I came into the possession of a book written by Marvin O'lasky, **"The Tragedy of American Compassion".** It proved to be a very interesting book and the results of this tragedy are being manifested big time in America today. The poverty of mentality is bearing some bitter fruit in all levels and areas of our nation today and will only proceed to get worse if not checked immediately by the implementation of much Godly wisdom, knowledge, and understanding, as well as intelligence and common sense, all of which are in terribly short supply in our world today. Many are the evil inventions of mankind in evidence today, some old, some new, which include "political correctness" that has replaced the absolutes of Biblical truths. Then we have the new concepts of "tolerance ", which proposes the embracing of everything and anything that is contrary to Biblical values, and "diversity", which accompanies tolerance in the attempted forcing of diversifying in the direction of whatever opposes Biblical principles, truth, and absolutes.

Thus is the foundation of our nation slowly crumbling beneath the weight of adversities being imposed by many of our "own countrymen" who are American citizens but conduct themselves contrary to foundational American practices based on Biblical principles and values. Unfortunately we haven't had any leaders who have the clout, courage, or intestinal fortitude [get, grit, and guts] to unite together and bring an end to such atrocities or stand alone if none will stand with them. All they can do is discuss the problems and blame someone else for them. If they spent their time, effort, and finances in fixing the problems rather than attempting to fix the blame, we might see some amazing results, however, **[Genesis 6:5]: "And God saw** that the wickedness of man was great in the earth and that every imagination of the thoughts of his heart was only evil continually". Thus are we burdened by our lack of knowledge, [Hosea 4:6-7].

These "buck passers" not only cause multitudes of problems but are very adamant in fixing the blame on others. *They are indeed of "their father the devil who is a liar and the father of it, and an accuser of the brethren" and anyone else they can lay or "fix" the blame on for the problems at hand,* [John 8:44]-[Revelation 12:10]. Is it any wonder they perish forever without even having the common sense and enough intelligence to regard, or question the reasons why they are perishing and search for some solutions to the prevailing idiocy. And it hasn't changed; neither have we learned from the bumps on the heads of the past nor our own lumps of the present. We can build super smooth highways to drive our automobiles on but the pathways of life remain full of disastrous lumps, bumps, chuckholes, and ruts of disaster because we are suffering from nationwide and worldwide poverty of soul and mentality. [3 John 2] "Beloved, I wish above all things that you mayest prosper and be in good health, EVEN AS THY SOUL PROSPERTH", [Romans 12:2] "And be not conformed to this world: but be ye transformed by the renewing of your mind, that ye may prove what is that good, and acceptable, and perfect will of God".

There is certainly a close correlation between our souls, spirits, minds, and hearts, or what is referred to as the inner or new man, renewed and in the process of being [Revelation 4:11], "re-created in the image and likeness of Christ and a resurrection of his excellency within us". It is absolutely amazing what God in his love and mercy has provided for us through Jesus Christ our Saviour and Lord in spite of the fact that we are so undeserving. It's an amazing thing, this love and grace of God and we don't even have to understand it to receive and enjoy it; *just accept it.* We who have availed ourselves of this vast abundance of provision, available only through Jesus, **have only begun to see and enjoy that which presently and ultimately awaits us as we continue to diligently seek and serve him in faith with joyfulness and gladness of heart for the abundance of all things, [Hebrews 11:6]-[Deuteronomy 28:47]-[1 Corinthians 2:9-10]-[Ephesians 2:7].** He is consistently re-enforcing the truth of his word to us through his word, his present and eternal provision of goodness and rewards to those who love, praise, worship, and serve him **"with the whole heart", [Psalms 119: 2, 10, 58].**

If there only existed a possibility of the fulfillment of this fact, it would be well worth the effort and life involved to pursue it unto attainment. Intelligence and wisdom will demand this, faith, trust, and hope will pursue it, and Almighty God through Jesus Christ will fulfill it; knowledge and understanding will result from it to the fulfilling of **"life and life more abundantly through Jesus Christ our Lord, who is the way, the truth, and the life". [Ephesians 3:19], "And to know the love of Christ, which passeth knowledge, that ye, that's us, may be filled with all the fullness of God", for today, tomorrow, and forever.** Thank you Father, for such an overwhelming abundance of eternal blessing.

When God has given us the gift of eternal, abundant life, and a man perishes, it is because he has chosen to do so. **[Deuteronomy 30:19] "I call heaven and earth to record this day against you, that I have set before you life and death, blessing and cursing: therefore choose life, that both you and your seed, descendents, may live".** If a man and his descendents perish, it could well be the fault of this man who rejected God's counsel to "choose life and blessing", and instead preferred death and cursing as his choice, choosing rather to enjoy **"the pleasure of sins for a season' [Hebrews 11: 25].**

It may sound rough, it may sound tough, it may sound crude and insensitive, it may even to some sound "un-Christian-like, but regardless, it has to be the absolute height of stupidity to thus choose against the knowledge of God and His eternal provisions for those who love and serve Him; and showing sympathy and compassion for such stupidity is out of the question. As our politicians campaigning for political advantage continue to tell us: *its time for a change,* they just don't realize what the needed change consists of. **[Hosea 4:6] "My people, any people, all people, are destroyed for lack of knowledge: because thou hast rejected knowledge, I will also reject thee, that thou shalt be no priest to me: seeing thou hast forgotten the law, word, of thy God, I will also reject thy children".**

Once again, we see the emphasis of the influence of the parents, good or bad, affecting and being passed on to the children. This influence of the parents has to revert back to, and include, whoever and whatever has imposed governing power of influence and conditioning on these young people. We as a nation, people, and whole societies alike that allow the imposition of contrary evil, un-Godly influence to so affect these young ones have to shoulder the responsibility of the impending results. This does not, however, release the individual so affected from the responsibility of personal correction of contrary behavioral inconsistencies in their own life.

Somebody, nevertheless, has to teach them: enter government, with its various manifestations and God ordained responsibilities and duties of encouraging and protecting the teaching of Biblical principles and standards for the benefit of the individuals and all those who they will influence and affect unto the entire society. If this is for good, the society benefits, however if government disregards its responsibilities and duties, the society continues in a destructive mode without the knowledge that would prevent its destruction. If governments, individuals, and societies can reclaim the condition commonly referred to as "common sense"; this will help, but there doesn't seem to be enough common sense left in this world, indeed this nation, to have much positive affect on our American society anymore.

It would seem that at first glance, all that has to do with positive, intelligent mental capabilities has fallen victim to such things as "political correctness, toleration, relativity, diversity, "separation of church and state", etc, for the purpose of the separation of God and people, and whatever other "evil invention" the despisers of God and the nominal church can conjure up. **These things are all reminiscent of " the gates of hell" which SHALL NOT prevail against the church of [Matthew 16:18], that Jesus in building in the hearts and lives of the "few there be that find the strait gate and narrow way that leads to life and life eternal", [Matthew 7:14].** Children had parents before "government" was officially established to govern. These parents received direction and commandments for such teaching, training, or governing authority long before any formal established tribe, state, national, or whatever organization was founded to govern, guide direct, and protect. As groups, tribes, families, whatever, grew larger it became necessary for the establishing and appointing of qualified individuals to assist in the governing of such groups.

None of these groups were ever intended to govern in opposition to God and his righteousness, but to assist in accordance with God's will and ways. Herein lay the problem, if they were to do things God's ways they had to think the way he thought. But being given free moral agency, they went astray according to their own "pernicious ways" due to the evil nature of man that has always been at war with God's righteousness **even when it is beneficial to them as individuals to conform**

to God's thoughts and ways, [Isaiah 55: 8]. I've heard it said that man is an intelligent being. I would have to take issue with that statement, as I don't see much evidence of that in the general populace as well as in our governmental structure. I do witness some in the Christian world but there is room for much more of it even there. And I suppose God would like to see more of it manifested in that area too. There is no doubt that God created man as an intelligent being, after all he made him in his own image and likeness, but it didn't take long for man to mess that up. When God told man that in the day that he disobeyed him, "thou shalt surely die", I do believe his intelligence was one of the first casualties and man hasn't been able to reclaim it since to an acceptable degree.

This intelligence must have begin to diminish a bit before he took his "bite out of the apple" or he wouldn't have done it to begin with. Then again, considering the fact there was a woman involved in the situation: she may have had a negative effect on his intelligence being operative in positive fashion as has been known to happen, providing there was any intelligence left at all. Many a good man has lost his head over a "skirt" and as I have been given to understand, she didn't even have one on at the time. In **[Genesis 2:17]** Adam was given strict instruction not to eat of **"the tree of the knowledge of good and evil, for that in the day that thou eatest thereof thou shalt surely die".** Did he indeed die? The Bible says he lived nine hundred-thirty years. That's not bad for a guy that was supposed to die the day he ate of the tree of the knowledge of good and evil. There certainly is much spiritual application to be made here, which of course the world cannot understand. This is probably one of the situations that the scoffers, scorners, and skeptics try to use to prove the many contradictions they claim are in the Bible. There is something involved here that is of much greater importance than a body fashioned out of the dust of the ground.

Let's consider Adams brain, his mind, his intelligence factor. I have heard it said that a person only uses a very small percentage of their brain; opinions seem to vary somewhat as to the amount, so it's really impossible to know whether or not any of the experts really know what they are talking about. Given the fact that man was made in the image and likeness of God, it would seem that there was originally an intelligence there that is not manifesting itself today. Is this what God was referring to when he said, **"for in the day that thou eatest thereof, thou shalt surly die"?** Certainly the conduct of man every since that time has not been befitting of a Godly directed intelligence in its operation. Adam abdicated his dominion authority and power, his Godly image, likeness and excellency, **[Job 4:21]** to the devil. Though we say he was stupid to do that, we have been doing it every since. All Adam had to do was start the ball rolling and man has kept it going with ever increasing intensity since it all started, **[Hosea 4:7], "As they were increased, so they sinned against me: therefore will I change their glory into shame".**

God gave us Jesus to reconcile us back to himself through repentance of sin and believing the gospel unto obedience, returning to us that which the devil stole by deception from Adam. We do not really seem to understand the significance of what happened on that old rugged cross and in the tomb from which Jesus was resurrected unto life. Judging from the general condition of humanity, I will have to agree on the "brain" experts, conceding to the fact that man does use a very small amount of his brain, how much, I don't know nor do I really care. Certainly it is evident especially in the pursuit of Godly wisdom, knowledge, understanding, intelligence, and common sense that the percentage left in operation is extremely small compared to what it was originally.

This intelligence factor in its relationship with God and his divine nature defines who and what a person is. Physical prowess doesn't really count for much in God's eyes. It didn't help Goliath any when he was up against a small shepherd boy who knew how to trust in God and walk with him. Goliath won a lot of battles when he was up against men who were walking in the ways of the world where men of the world naturally walked, but when he met a man walking in the Spirit of God it was a different story. We have a lot of Goliath's in this world that represent "gates of hell", but none in the kingdom of God, **the [Matthew 16:18] church of Jesus Christ.**

Here's where we need the David's who know how to trust in God to smash the gates of hell as more than conquerors through Christ. We are desperately in need of *"mighty men of valor"* to lay their lives on the line for the King of Kings, fearless and ready to sacrifice all for the cause of the gospel of Jesus Christ. There are a few that have done that, but not necessarily in this nation in our modern and post-modern days as we are to accustomed to our creature comforts to risk them. It does seem as there needs to be a change in attitudes as to who is in charge of the facts concerning humanity, and the truth of the reality of God and his fullness. It is time to present all this as fact that has already been established and proven by God himself from the beginning of time and put the anti-God elements in the position of defending their faith in the nothingness and hopelessness of their arguments that present nothing whatsoever that is of value or benefit to themselves, the rest of mankind, or God.

If people wish to present an argument concerning what they believe in, at least argue in favor of something that has enough value in it to justify the time and energy involved in the argument. So far as God is concerned, he is established: let the opposition defend their position, providing you wish to waste your time listening to them. They make about as much sense as a dogs incessant barking at the moon in the middle of the night. There must be a point somewhere in that about them making all their noise of opposition and ignorance in darkness, barking at the light. But they insist on continuing with their incessant noise making in their persistent pursuit of pointlessness. These are among they who **"are destroyed from morning to evening: they perish for ever without any regarding it, their excellency that is in them goes away and they die, even without wisdom", [Job 4:20-21].** These are those who, against direct counsel, have chosen death and cursing in preference to life and blessing, **who are destroyed for lack of knowledge and their children with them because of their rebellion and disobedience, [Deuteronomy 30:19]-Hosea 4:6]. Indeed has Shakespeare spoken the truth when he said "What fools ye mortals be".**

NOTES

VII.   EMPHASIS

I have heard it said that it is not what we teach, but what we "EMPHASIZE" in our teaching that matters. I believe it was a sports coach from whom that theory first originated, who it was I do not know. I suspect however, that it was Vince Lombardi who coached the Green Bay Packers to greatness. The idea does, regardless of from whom it originated, have much merit. The Bible is, in its totality, because of its message of truth, provision of entire, over all well-being of all creation, and the salvation and deliverance of all humanity from the destructive elements and results of sin and iniquity, worthy of intense study and diligent application. Another concept, I understand originated with Mr. Lombardi, was that practice doesn't make perfect; **"perfect" practice makes perfect.** Certainly the Word of God, with all its provisions and other considerations, is definitely worthy of **"perfect practice".** We must train our minds to move within the confines and directives of God's Word. **"Thus do we live and move and have our being in him"**, **[Acts 17: 28]**, **"our minds are renewed, and hearts diligently kept"**, **[Romans 12: 2]; [Proverbs 4:23],** being directed by God's counsel of righteousness, instead of the erroneous counsel and ways of this world.

There are, nevertheless, certain scriptures, that in the interest of direct response to the message of redemption and reconciliation of man, counseling man to Christian maturity, and back to God for intimacy of relationship; need to be "emphasized", the two scriptures above being included. **[2 Timothy 3:16-17]** is just such scripture that reveals purpose and necessity of the inclusion of all scripture in our lives for consideration and application. **"All scripture is given by inspiration of God, and is profitable for doctrine, for reproof, for correction, for instruction in righteousness:**

that the man of God may be perfect, *thoroughly furnished unto all good works". Within this total framework of the Bible we find scriptures that are directed to the calling of mankind through the person of Jesus Christ to repent of his sin, accept, and be obedient to God's plan of salvation, redemption, and restoration to an intimacy of fellowship with God himself.

After this process is in place within a person's life for its continuation of development and enrichment, there is no end of scriptures found throughout God's word provided to assist, counsel and direct the new Christian in this continuation of spiritual growth and development unto maturity. At this point I would like to say something that may put some within my Christian family at odds with me concerning the subject and provision of God's "amazing grace". I am sure we can, or should, all agree that we are saved by this grace of God. We do, however, live, grow, develop, mature and move in him by studying his word and obedience to it. Thus is our position within this application of God's grace and abiding presence, secure and with continuing development for his pleasure and our own eternal well-being.

Let's explore some of these "need to emphasize" scriptures that will be of such everlasting importance in our developmental relationship with our God. Let me say here that I have a profound and deep respect and love for the Word of God, The Holy Bible. God has, however, been working under an extreme handicap throughout the ages as he has enlisted the help of the only source available for the job that needed to be accomplished. He has enlisted man to do the required task at hand and entrusted him to do it correctly. If God ever made a mistake, this was probably it. God seems to imply this in several areas of scripture, **[Genesis 5: 5-13],** being a prime example of how God regards man with his incessant propensity for sin and iniquity. It's not a matter of "love the sinner, but hate the sin". It is a matter of the vessel insisting on keeping and operating within its cargo of rebellion and disobedience that requires its removal, The remedy for this is found in **[1 Thessalonians 4: 1-7], note verse 4, "That every one of you should [both], know how to, [and] possess his vessel in sanctification and honour".** I have found that knowing how to do something and actually doing it are two entirely different things. Once again, **"perfect practice makes perfect", [Lombardi 1: 1].**

Because of this mans rebellion, disobedience, abominations, iniquities, and filth; God justifiably determined to exterminate him but was stopped by "a man" in three different occasions. Nevertheless, man continues to make many mistakes along life's way. Thank God for his amazing grace, love and forgiveness, conditioned, and administered of course, on our repentance of whatever transgression or transgressions that need to be repented of. Some of these mistakes are not necessarily classed as sin, such as using a poorly chosen word in a Bible translation, which may lead to a rather erroneous misunderstanding of a Biblical truth. It does in no way imply or mean the truth is diminished or compromised in any way; it just leads to some misunderstanding which can be corrected with some additional study and Bible counsel. I too, need this additional, continued, and I stress, continued, Holy Spirit counsel and guidance, correction, and direction on a daily and sometimes hourly basis and enjoy it immensely. Gaining new knowledge about God and finding new discoveries in the treasure of his word is not only exiting but is, **[3 John: 2], "profitable to the soul"** and continued well-being of one's self and all those who are exposed to such discoveries and knowledge.

I have been leading up to one of my pet peeves in what I consider a poorly chosen word to project a beautiful truth, but does not fit well within the context of the message that it attempts to convey. That word is "fear", acceptable in some areas but terribly misused in others. However in the process of such leading I have inadvertently stumbled over another area or word that has, in its use, been a source of some confusion and misunderstanding in some teaching. That area is on the subject and use of the word "self". Please bear in mind that the position from which I speak is based on my own perceptions and conceptions and does in no way imply that those with which I disagree are incorrect in their summations. They simply speak from their own positions of understanding and perceptions, and they may well be correct. This just reflects that to which they have been exposed, conditioned, and taught over their life's span up to this point in time. It is only that I respectfully disagree with some of the things I hear, but continue to love my family in spite of any differences of opinions. Let's address this subject of "self" and then go back to the questionable use of the word "fear" as it is used and applied in some areas.

I have heard over the years the phrase "you have to get self out of the way, or, you have to crucify "self". Even though this all sounded so churchy and spiritual it never made any sense to me because my "self" is all I had to operate and work with. I began to question if they even knew what they were talking about or just wanted or tried to sound spiritual by saying something that had a kind of spiritual ring to it. I really don't consider myself as a rebel but I do have a rather questioning, inquisitive, mind and I needed to know that if what they were telling me was somewhat incorrect, or was correct. Thank God for his wonderful Holy Spirit that was sent to comfort, teach, direct, correct us, and bring all things to our remembrance. What a valuable, absolutely essential source of strength and enlightenment he is as he directs us through heavens own schoolroom of education with the Bible as his textbook of information, inspiration, and revelation.

Through this do we grow in the grace and knowledge of our Lord and Saviour Jesus Christ and our Father in Heaven,

Almighty God. It didn't take long before my thoughts were directed to **[James 4:7]**, to just a portion of that scripture that says, **"Submit yourselves therefore to God"**. The scripture continues on but this is what I needed to begin to unravel the question of what to do with my "self". Obviously this scripture is directed to all, thus the plural use of "yourselves". Being an individual among the multitudes, I have to apply this in the singular which would naturally be; **"Submit thy "self" therefore to God"**. This immediately made sense to me as I knew from **[Genesis 1:26]** that God initially created man in his image and likeness and from **[Job 4: 21]** there was an excellency designed within this creation, the significance of which is yet to be discovered, explored and, yes, resurrected; an excellency that is contained within this likeness of God of which up to this time we virtually know nothing about.

It came as a wonderful truth that this "self" that God created, though scarred with sin was to be submitted to God through his divine provision of Jesus Christ that he might take it and **re-create it [Rev 4:11], renew it [Romans 12:2], and reconcile it [2 Corinthians 5:17-18], to himself as a new creature in our Lord Jesus Christ, saved by his wonderful amazing grace for his glory, honor, and pleasure.** So what was the problem? It was not, it is not "self", but "selfishness", a sinful condition that must be crucified and destroyed before and in the process of "submitting ourselves to God through whole heartedly repenting of the iniquity that is "found" in us and accepting of Jesus Christ as Saviour and Lord". I have heard it said that selfishness is the root cause of all sin. Considering all the ways, if we were able to do so, [it is more experienced than ever regarded or considered], selfishness being manifested by a sinful nature.

This concept of the connection of selfishness and sin certainly needs our attention and study. It is no wonder that it must be destroyed lest it destroy us. At any rate this short article on the subject of self and selfishness may prove of interest to the reader and I sincerely hope that it will inspire you to further exploration and discoveries of your own. There are a great many other scriptures that can well be emphasized, applied and used in your journey of discovery of Biblical truths.

Now to the subject of fear and to it's use in relation to the normal, natural, way that humanity views and relates to it. There are many different words in both the Hebrew and Greek languages that give many different shades and applications of meaning to the word fear. I am more interested at this point in time as to how the word "fear" is generally perceived and applied by the general public and their response or reaction to it. There are many places in the Bible where the use of the word "fear" as is generally interpreted by humanity as to be frightened, afraid, scared, or to feel panic or terror in its correct usage.

It is amazing that the word "fear" also has within its scope of meaning, but to the other side of the spectrum, the word "reverence", or to have a reverential awe or adoration of God. This meaning or rendition is more in line with and conducive to the many admonitions to **"love the Lord thy God with all thy heart, with all thy soul, with all thy strength, with all thy might etc"**. There are many scriptures where this command is stated in various wordings and arrangements. **[Matthew 22:38-40]** gives this as the first and great commandment with the second commandment like unto it, **"thou shalt love thy neighbor as thyself"**. In reference to the above section on "self"; if our "self" is so despicable so as to be cast aside and gotten out of the way, why is it used as an example of how we are to love our neighbors? At any rate "love" is the theme of these two "emphasized" commandments on which **"hang all the law and the prophets"** and the thought of fear definitely does not fit in here. Love and reverence flow together quite nicely and are complimentary while love and the common thought, idea, and understanding of fear are totally incompatible. **[1John 4:18-21] vs.18 "There is no fear in love; but perfect love casteth out fear: because fear hath torment. He that feareth is not made perfect in love." Vs.19 "We love him, reverence, worship and adore him because he first loved us".** There can be no room for fear, or even the implication of it in a relationship that is dependant on love, friendship, devotion and intimacy etc.

Before Adam's sin he walked and talked in the Garden in a beautiful relationship with God. It was only after his disobedience and rebellion he hid himself in fear. If you are living with sin in your life there is definitely room for fear of God, and a basic intelligence would demand it. However, Jesus has made provision for us to come back into the Garden to walk and talk in intimacy of the fellowship of redemption, reconciliation and unity that God himself, because of his great love for us, made available to us, through his Son Jesus our Lord, the first among many brethren. Fear, as generally understood in our world today has no part with that or the facilitating of it. Indeed the perfect love of God for us, if we realize, accept, and walk in the light of this love casts out fear, and we can walk and talk in the garden of intimate communion with God once again in total reconciliation to him. There are decisions that each one of us will have to make along the way to make this all possible. Thank you Jesus for making it all available to us.

Now that I have pretty well covered a couple of my pet peeves maybe we can get on with some scriptures that need to be emphasized along with our general teaching. Many of these scriptures will refer directly to the two words "self and fear" just covered. There is a word that appears many times throughout the Bible which makes general reference to specific things that must be ferreted out by the individual to get to the root of what is being referred to. That word is in itself "things".

For instance in **[Hebrews 6:9]; But beloved, we are persuaded better "things" of you, and "things" that accompany salvation, though we thus speak,** *or are to be emphasized and practiced* to be affective in our daily living. We have two references here to "things". What are these "things" specifically that are so generally referred to that seem to refer back to the previous verses of chapter 6? What are these "things" that accompany salvation? In the first "things" the writer(s) here seem to be referring to are a steadfastness and stability in God, not being guilty of the transgressions mentioned in verses 4-6 and 8. There seems to be a direct correlation between vs.7 and **[Psalms 1:2-3]** concerning the taking in of nourishment from a steady direct contact with the living waters of the Word through being **"planted by it, delighting in it, meditating in it day and night" and [Psalms 119:165], "loving the Word".** Because of this, this person is fruitful and prosperous, receiving blessings from God. I will leave that where it is and encourage the readers, whoever they may eventually be, to explore that further for themselves. It simply comes down to the fact; if you wish to be like the person of verse3, DO WHAT IT SAYS IN VERSE 2. This will start you on a lifelong journey of exploration to discover the treasures of God's Word that lead to life and life more abundantly.

Now let's go on to the "things" that accompany salvation. What could these things be? In my earlier years within the Pentecostal movement it seemed to be generally understood that if you were saved, obtained your salvation, and were baptized with the Holy Spirit, you pretty well had it all put together. Now I find through my own personal study of the word there are some additional "things" required, not necessarily for salvation but to "accompany" the salvation experience, enriching it and **[Titus 2:10], "showing all good fidelity and adorning the doctrine of God our Saviour in all "things".** This concept of our being charged with the prospect of "adorning" the doctrine of God is a rather interesting thought, and the adorning of it in all "things" makes one wonder what these "things" could be. Let's go back to **[Deuteronomy 28: 45&47] and see if a part of this adorning might consist of vs.45, in our hearkening unto the voice of the Lord our God to keep his word, his principles, his statutes and commandments, vs.47, serving the Lord our God with joyfulness, and with gladness of heart for the abundance of all things.** Lets not forget [Isaiah 64:7] and the challenge to call **upon the name of the Lord our God and "stir up ourselves to take hold of him"** in willing obedience by seeking out, DILIGENTLY applying, and **doing always those "things" that please him, following the example of Jesus in [John 8:29] and enjoying his constant presence as a result.**

Many of the "things" that adorn the doctrine of God, that please him, and accompany salvation are the same "things". We won't find out what these things are though unless we **[2 Timothy 2:15], "study to show ourselves approved unto God, workmen that needeth not to be ashamed, rightly dividing the word of truth" and, [Acts 10:35] fearing, [revering], God and working righteousness, thus being accepted with him.** In our studies we most certainly will have to include **[Galatians 5:22-23], the "Fruit of the Spirit"** as having a prominent place among those "things" needed in our walk with the Lord in this **new and living way, [Hebrews 10: 20].** What about the **[Philippians 4:8-9] "things" we are to think on in the process of [Romans 12:2] renewing our minds and [Proverbs 4: 23], keeping our heart with all diligence so that it will issue forth life** instead of death that issues, *or radiates* forth from the heart that is not kept and guarded diligently within the confines and counsel of the word of Gods truth that sets men and nations free.

These "things" that we are commanded to think on are the very "things" that will facilitate and make possible the "renewing of the mind", delivering it from conformity to the world that is opposed to God and his righteousness. We find direct reference to these "things" in **[2 Corinthians 10:4-5]**. The thoughts here to a large degree infer a collection of renewed minds made mighty through God, thinking his thoughts, and producing ways that conform to God's ways. These ways are the ways of casting down evil, contrary, vain, etc, imaginations, [thinking-thoughts] and every [other] high thing [or low, despicable things] that qualifies as a gate of hell and exalts itself in an attempt to prevail against the **[Matthew 16:18] church of Jesus Christ and the knowledge of God.**

If a person is really serious about "bringing into captivity every thought to the obedience of Christ" and everyone professing Christianity must be actively pursuing this, then the constant blending together of one's life with, and walking in the **[Psalms 1:1-3] Godly counsel of his word, delighting in it, and meditating in it day and night is an absolute** necessity. This is the only way you can ever attain to being the person alluded to in vs. 3. If you wish to enjoy the presence of the God of peace, you must discipline your mind unto renewal by **thinking on these "things", [Philippians 4: 8-9].** If you wish to enjoy **great peace** with victory over potential and actual stumbling blocks and offences, you must learn to **"love" the Word of God, [Psalms 119:165].** If you desire to have and enjoy the **perfect peace** that proceeds from the Father, you must train your mind to be **"stayed on him and trust in him" [Isaiah 26:3].**

The few scriptures that have been mentioned here in these pages are very few in comparison to the many that are so very essential in the process of developing a renewed mind, in the diligent keeping of the heart that brings forth life through the words of a Bible orientated Holy Spirit taught, **well disciplined**

tongue, [Proverbs 25: 11], and walking in this [Hebrew 10: 20], "new and living way". It is my deepest desire and with a sincere hope that these scriptures will become the few among many that you will emphasize in your general exploration and study of God's Word as you avail yourself of all the "things" that God **by his divine power has given us that pertain to life and Godliness, [2 Peter 1:3-4]; becoming by his great and precious promises, partakers of his divine nature.**

As I bring this brief summary of the overall abundance of God's Word with some scriptures that need to be emphasized, there are many others, to a close, allow me to leave with you as a departing gesture. **[Hebrews 13: 20-21], "Now the God of peace, that brought again from the dead our Lord Jesus, that great shepherd of the sheep, through the blood of the everlasting covenant, Make you perfect in every good work to do his will, working in you that which is well pleasing in his sight, through Jesus Christ; to whom be glory and dominion for ever and ever, Amen".** May you faithfully follow the leading of the Holy Spirit as he leads, teaches and guides you in your Biblical studies and explorations. I can't make your choices for you, neither can I do your reading, studying, and learning for you. You'll have to do it for your SELF. **[John 14: 26], "But the Comforter, which is the Holy Ghost, whom the Father will send in my name, he shall teach you all things, and bring all things to your remembrance whatsoever I have said unto you".**

Over the years I have become aware of different individuals developing various concepts and ideas in interpretations and views of scriptures. Recently my attention was drawn to a word I had never heard of before, there still remains a great many of them. I run on to them quite often which necessitates my keeping a couple of dictionaries close by for some essential illumination and enrichment of my rather limited uneducated abundance of knowledge in this area. The word "preterist" which refers to a person who is a preterit is what the one person was referring to the other person as being. Who these individuals are is not nearly as important as learning what the meaning of this word was. When I first ran across the word, having a bit of a suspicious mind, I immediately wondered, what new brand of sinner is this as the word has a rather ominous ring to it. I soon realized a preterit is not necessarily a sinner or saint, but just someone who had a different idea about certain things we are faced with from time to time in our Bible studies concerning a belief that certain events were not necessarily future but already past. Any how the way it was presented, without explanation of meaning, had a kind of sinister somewhat "accusation of discrepancy" sound to it. Regardless, the debate over these issues in question, plus others that arise from time to time, seem to be continuing among people who seem to have a need to express their opinions and make them known and get them across to others for whatever purpose they have in mind that may give them a sense of satisfaction.

At any rate there seems to be a rather extensive amount of time, effort, and energy, in the process wasted in majoring on minors. Who is right versus who is wrong in so many of these issues is unimportant considering the individuals have a tendency to both be wrong in taking the time and space to prove their point of view when neither one is going to have an effect on changing God's agenda for humanity nor enriching a persons relationship with our Lord and our God. On the contrary, such time, effort, and life spent in such pursuits robs people caught up in such activities of valuable time that could be used for deepening their Biblically taught and required relationship with God and each other.

Satan continues to be very subtle and successful in his robbing techniques as he goes about his devouring activities, **[John 10: 10], [1 Peter 5: 8].** Unfortunately, many well meaning Christians are unwittingly conned into assisting him. It is through this process that unity is wounded and many "gates of hell" are formed in the redeemed community of Christ by the redeemed themselves, and the church suffers as a result. We have all been witnesses to these abominations through church splits, bitterness, animosity, etc, etc; not necessarily across denominational boundaries, but within denominations themselves.

What a tragedy and how it must grieve God to see his people in such a state of foolishness as they inadvertently choose death and cursing rather than life and blessing, **[Deuteronomy 30: 19],** and do so within church settings. And the robber continues to insidiously steal, to kill, and destroy because the people fail to be sober and vigilant, keeping their heart with all diligence so their hearts can issue forth life to each other and a lost and dying world, and we lose so many of our young people by our erroneous and unbiblical examples. What good is accomplished to win a battle of arguments when in so doing you assist the enemy in losing the war for the souls? **[Matthew 16:26; Mark 8: 36; Luke 9: 25], "What doth it profit a man to gain the whole world, and lose his own soul",** or be guilty in contributing to the loss of others?

There are many commandments that we need to emphasize in our daily Christian life and living, commandments that we need to keep at the forefront of our consciousness and awareness. To set the stage for this consider, **[Matthew 22: 36-40], "Master, which is the great commandment in the law? Jesus said unto him, Thou shalt love the Lord thy God with all thy heart, and with all thy soul, and with all thy mind. This is the first and great commandment. And the second is like unto it, Thou shalt love thy neighbor as thy self. *On these two commandments hang all the law and the prophets".*** All the rest of the Bible is contained within these scriptures in all its implications and applications. This is where we apply some "Bible Biology", dissecting and studying each word, how it interacts and relates to the words around it, what its various meanings are in other portions of scripture, and how they work together to magnify and reveal God and His divine nature. The Bible is God's textbook: He, through the person of the Holy Spirit is our perfect and able teacher and instructor in righteousness, **[John 14: 26],** but we have to do our own studying and learning, **[2 Timothy 2: 15].**

NOTES

NOTES

VIII.   FURNISHING YOUR HOUSE

Any activity, be it mental, spiritual, or physical, they all go together with your mentality; thinking and thoughts leading the way that would tend to life, or if in opposition to God, place a person in a position of God's judgment and inviting death and destruction. Considering the fact that God is the giver of life; the establishing, building, and maintenance of such life must be according to his specifications and instructions as he is the only one qualified to give these specifications and instructions which he has, in these last days, made known to us through his only begotten Son Jesus Christ as recorded in his Word, The Holy Bible, **[Hebrews 1: 1-2]**. Any choice of opposition and rebellion against this giver of life in violation of his will, Word, and ways, would not only be unwise but just plain stupid, **[Deuteronomy 30:19].** You may call a person a sinner and not get much reaction as most people realize that they are sinners, but call them stupid and they are ready to fight. The problem is that people don't acquaint sinning with stupidity. You can do stupid things that won't necessarily be sinning, but you can't sin without embracing stupidity in its most gross destructive forms.

God is very kind, but depending on our choices in relationship to his will and desires, can be the God of wrath and judgment but generally manifesting a host of other Godly qualities within his divine nature that are commensurate with his kindness before wrath and judgment are administered as **"he is not willing that any should perish, but that all should come to repentance"**, **[2 Peter 3:9].** God, in his kindness and goodness doesn't use the descriptive word "stupid", but refers to people in rebellion and their conduct in such terms as, "fool, foolish, foolishly, foolishness, fool's, and fools. However to search out the depth of what it is to be a "fool", or conduct oneself foolishly, a person may well desire to be, only "stupid" on occasion rather than spending an entire lifetime as a fool. Even intelligent people do stupid things on occasion; been there, done that; but to exist continually in that condition, never advancing beyond the existence of being a fool, when such means are so available for such advancement, is the height of stupidity.

The "prodigal son" lived in his fathers house with his father's provision, began thinking, having thoughts like a fool that led him into an existence of stupidity that ultimately drove him destitute, into the pigpens of this world. There he remained until his thinking and thoughts began to change concerning his fathers "goodness" in comparison to his own waywardness and stupidity. This led him to a decision borne out of his desperate state of despair to "repent" and return to his fathers house, confess his sin and ask his fathers forgiveness. Somewhere in this mental process before he even physically left the pigpen existence, the beginning of wisdom began to take shape as he acknowledged his fathers goodness and began to give him reverence. The word "unwise" is used in reference to this foolishness of fools, the one's who refuse to search out and avail themselves of the available means to the intelligent end of salvation, redemption, and reconciliation through Jesus Christ our Lord. **[Proverbs 1:7], "The fear of the Lord is the beginning of knowledge: but fools despise wisdom and instruction."** *This refers both to the "leaders," and followers alike.*

Being voted in, appointed to, or otherwise attaining to a "leadership" position does not automatically endow a person with the necessary qualifications of wisdom, knowledge, understanding, intelligence, and whatever else may be required to function within, and execute that particular leadership position properly. There is certainly a tremendous lack of wisdom, knowledge, understanding, and intelligence, as well as simple common sense, being manifested in our world today as evidenced by the absence of it; perpetrated by the erroneous thinking, thoughts, with the resultant conversation and conduct of the people involved, including our great nation of America. So much for post-modern, anti-God, anti-Bible mentality! I am so very thankful that my relationship with God is on a personal basis, not being dependent on others, and of the overall condition of the society and culture I am living in.

Before I proceed further, I feel it a necessity to identify the God I am referring to as the God of the Bible, the God of Israel, of Abraham, Isaac, and Jacob, the God of creation. With all the religions that are present with all their gods, god has pretty much become a generic term, so without specifics for identification you may be mistaken as to which, God, god, or gods are being referred to. He may be further identified by the use of the name, Jehovah, or the Jewish, Yahweh, but this should be sufficient for the purpose of identification. It is of extreme importance here to include the name of Jesus Christ, **[Acts 4:10-12], "for there is none other name under heaven given among men, whereby we must be saved".** This Jesus, **[John 1:14], "the glory as of the only begotten of the Father, full of grace and truth, given of God because of his love, that whosoever believeth in him should not perish, but have everlasting life",[John3:16], is the only door to the sheepfold of God, [John 10:1-18].** He is the foundation of the gospel message that the apostle Paul speaks of to the Corinthians, **[1 Corinthians 3:10-11],** unto salvation, being reconciled back into the presence of the Father.

[Psalms 127:1] "Except the Lord build the house, they labor in vain that build it." What is this "house"? It is any endeavor man undertakes, the most important being his own relationship with God through Jesus Christ, the way ,the truth, the life, and the door, who is himself, the foundation, the solid rock upon, and within which man must build and in which must be anchored all our endeavors. **[Matthew 7:24-25] "Therefore**

whosoever heareth theses sayings of mine, *and doeth them*, I will liken him unto a wise man, which built his house upon a rock: and the rain descended, and the floods came, and the winds blew, and beat upon that house; and it fell not: for it was founded upon a [the] rock". Your house is, your life, which we will consider here before we go on to other things because if your own "house" is not in order, you will adversely affect, unto destruction, everything around you that comes under your "out of order influence". This is the reason that it is so important that leaders, those in positions of authority, influence, and power have their own "houses in order" by **"doing all things decently an in order"**, **[1 Corinthians 14: 40]**, according to God's divine building instructions. If they be blind leaders, by reason of their positions of power and authority, they will influence and create blind followers, and both will fall into the ditch of destruction, **[Matthew 15:14]**. These are those described in **[Mathew 7:26-27]**, **"And every one that heareth these sayings of mine, and doeth them <u>not</u>, shall be likened unto a foolish man, which built his house upon the sand: and the rain descended, and the floods came, and the winds blew, and beat upon that house, and it fell: and great was the fall of it"**.

You might ask yourself, what does America today and this scripture reference have in common? It is absolutely essential that your "house", your life, and all that it entails; marriage, family, relationships, careers, etc, etc, be built according to God's specifications, his truth, counsel and absolutes, not according to man's wishy-washy sands of emotional self centered variableness, relativity, and undependability. It is only by building your house on God's foundation, Jesus Christ, the rock of **[Matthew 16:18]** that your "house" will be able to withstand the rains, floods, and winds, the storms of opposition that will certainly come, and remain unshakeable and unaffected, yet stronger, more solid and committed than ever. Be assured, the majority of the storms you will face as a committed Christian will be from the same source Paul experienced **[2 Corinthians 11:23-27], at the hands of "mine own countrymen".**

In **[1 Thessalonians 2:14-16]** it speaks of Christians suffering opposition and persecutions at the hands of "your own countrymen"; those that please not God, and are contrary to all men, *forbidding us to speak to the Gentiles that they might be saved.* It sounds like the idea of the "separation of church and state" has been around much longer than we realized. This certainly sounds like a preamble to it, reintroduced in our post-modern age by the anti-God element of "our own countrymen" who are desperately in need of Biblical instruction, including, **[2 Timothy 2: 25,], "those that oppose themselves".** Who indeed, are these, who in their arrogance, rebellion, and ignorance, have assumed some ridiculous pseudo authority to forbid men to speak to others about God, his glory and majesty unto salvation! These are not aliens or foreigners, but our own "countrymen" who consider themselves as patriotic Americans, who have formed some sort of legalized sham to choke off the flow, influence and Word of God from a society and culture that is being spiritually starved for God's Word because of this "separation of church and state" shutoff valve being initiated. Our danger does not come from foreign exterior terrorism, but from internal terrorism, legalized, lawful, forced, and intended separation of God and people that takes its first form as separation of church and state.

Our own countrymen are initiating the demise that will be the eventual destruction of America unless the people who are being led by the blind cast off their own blindness, rallying themselves to repentance, **[Isaiah 64: 7], "stir up themselves to take hold of God"** and restore Him to his rightful position as supreme commander in chief and Lord of all. We have His Word, His promise, and He cannot lie, **[2 Chronicles 7: 14], "If my people, which are called by my name, shall humble**

themselves, and pray, and seek my face, and turn from their wicked ways; then [not until then] will I hear from heaven, and will forgive their sins, and will heal their land". It does seem as though God has placed some conditions on his "hearing from heaven". These conditions are met in; humbling ourselves in repentance, [turning from our wicked ways, reinstating God as supreme ruler and his word as our personal and national constitution], praying and seeking God's face in obedience, and acceptance of Jesus Christ as Saviour and Lord. THEN he will hear from heaven, forgive our sins, and heal, assisting us in the rebuilding and restoring of our "houses," our lives, our families, our land and whatever else needs to be healed and **"recreated for his pleasure" [Revelation 4:11].** I have had some rather interesting thoughts concerning the relationship between man and the word of God. God has gone to considerable lengths, even to the extent of giving his son Jesus, as a once for all, for everyone, anyone, who will accept him, eternal sacrifice for sin. His instructions are simple and easy to understand, **[Deuteronomy 31:19], "I call heaven and earth to record this day against you, that I have set before you life and death, blessing and cursing: therefore choose life that both thou and thy seed may live."** He not only tells us which one to choose as God is smart enough to realize we don't seem to be intelligent enough to make that choice without guidance, but goes on to tell us why we should choose life and blessing.

If we really had a good understanding of what the glory of this "life and blessings" consisted of, and an equally good understanding of the extent and horrors of eternal hell contained, I don't think we would have nearly as difficult time in making the choice between the two. We however don't have this depth of understanding, and certainly not the knowledge of each, so God gives us what should be sufficient incentive for correct, intelligent, choice in our free moral judgment and selection. The addition of wisdom, beyond the "beginning of wisdom", along with a host of other things including the **knowledge that prevents destruction, [Hosea 4:6],** will be accumulated along the way provided we use that beginning of wisdom to prompt us to **[2 Timothy 2: 15-16], "Study to show thyself approved unto God, a workman that needeth not to be ashamed, rightly dividing the word of truth. Verse 16; But shun profane and vain babblings: for they will increase unto more ungodliness".** We don't hear much about the direction and counsel of verse 16 concerning profane and vain "babbling", but it makes for an interesting study as being one of the furnishings that is not desirable to have "in your house" and is something that proceeds from the abundance **[Luke 6: 45] of a heart that has *not* been "diligently kept", [Proverbs 4: 23], and a mind that *is not* renewed and transformed according to the counsel of God's word as taught by the Holy Spirit, [John 14: 26].**

I kind of got the impression that God was holding his word out to us and saying, Here is my word, live by obedience to it or die by disobedience to it. The choice is yours, I'm going fishing. I sort of chuckled over the simplicity of it until was directed to a scripture by, guess who, in **[Hosea 5:15], "I will go and return to my place, till they acknowledge their offence, and seek my face: in their affliction they will seek my early".** *Then as they initiate [2 Chronicles 7:14], doing what is required of them, I will fulfill my promise to them.* I would like to see that place. I've, as you can tell, have quite an active imagination, and I can see this place as a beautiful mountain range with crystal clear lakes and streams full of hungry trout and kokanee on some beautiful unspoiled, by man's idiocy, planet somewhere we know nothing about, which is why it's unspoiled. Time will tell whether I'm right or not, but it is a desire of my heart to visit that place with that beautiful log lodge he has up on a hillside overlooking one of those lakes. **[Revelation 21:7], "He that overcometh shall inherit all things: and I will be his God, and he shall be my** son." Don't tell me my desires, **[Psalms 37: 4]**, and dreams are out of reason, you just don't know my God. **"Delight thyself also in the Lord; and he shall give thee the desires of thine heart"**.

We find in **[1 Corinthians 2: 9-10]** some scripture concerning our future state and knowledge of it that is not generally nor specifically known, but is nevertheless available at God's discretion. **Vs.9, "But as it is written, Eye hath not seen, nor ear heard, neither have entered into the heart of man, the things which God hath prepared for them that love him. Vs.10, But God hath revealed them unto us by his Spirit: for the Spirit search all things, yea, the deep things of God."** It might be that God by his spirit has revealed such as this to my heart; time will tell, but after all, one of the main furnishings of my house is faith wherein I can relax in comfort, **"trusting the Lord and leaning not to my own understanding"**, **[Proverbs 5:5]. Again in [John 14:26], " But the Comforter, which is the Holy Ghost, whom the Father will send in my name, he shall teach you all things, and bring all things to your remembrance, whatsoever I have said unto you."** We must diligently study and embrace whatsoever he has to say unto us.

God has allowed me to build a room in my house [temple] to furnish with dreams and desires of a time well beyond the scope of this world and the wisdom of man, but in the promises of God and the hope he has set before us, to be administered at his discretion. There are many other furnishings in this house, or at least furnishings that God wants us to obtain, such as wisdom, knowledge, understanding, and intelligence. Then of course there is in **[Galatians 5:22-23], " the fruit of the Spirit, love, joy, peace, longsuffering, gentleness, goodness, faith, meekness, temperance: against such there is no law."** In **[2 Peter 1: 3-15]** is another list of essential furnishings, vs. 10, which, **"if you do these things, you shall never fall"**. Then of course we have the often mentioned but little exercised items such as **patience and forgiveness**. Some who have seen the value of these will exercise and furnish their house with them more than others. We have for the adorning and enhancing the beauty of our "house" the **"things that accompany salvation" [Heb. 6:9],** and the "things" that we can do that **"always please God" [John 8:29.]** These include the **"fearing, reverencing, of God and working of righteousness for acceptance with God", [Acts10: 35].**

If we put as much time, effort, thought, desire, interest etc, in the furnishing of our spiritual house as we do our material houses we would see our "standard of living" increase considerably; and a "more than enough" bank account would have little or nothing to do with it but may well be a result of it. This would facilitate the furnishings of peace, harmony, unity, and certainly the manifestations of love in our homes, things that wealth cannot buy.

Oh yes, lets not forget fellowship within the family of God. The art of this has been covered beneath the dust of neglect for so long it's hardly recognizable anymore. I myself feel a few pangs of guilt on this one. We have all become so busy in our own agendas that there is hardly room left for these spiritual necessities of the family and the furnishing of the home and heart. The demands and distractions of this material world on our time, lives, and finances raises a need for some serious re-evaluation about our priorities. **[Mark 8:36] "For what shall it profit a man, if he shall gain the whole world, and lose his own soul"?** It makes no difference if a man gains it or not if he wastes his life and time trying and never learning to **[Colossians 3:2] "set his affection on the things above, not on the things on the earth".** These things listed above are some of those "things" we need to "furnish our house" in order for it to remain on the Rock, the foundation, on which it was built.

In **[Isaiah 61:3]** we find some additional furnishings, **"beauty for ashes, the oil of joy for mourning, the garments of praise for the spirit of heaviness, that they might be called trees of righteousness, the planting of the Lord, that he might be glorified."** There are other furnishings to be found throughout the Bible, search them out, study them, implement them, exercise yourselves in them, furnish your house, God's temple with them; they are all characteristics of **the divine nature [2 Peter 1:4],** of which we are to be partakers of. **[Deuteronomy 4:9] "Only take heed to thyself, and keep thy soul diligently, that you [Ephesians 3:19] "might know the love of Christ, which passeth knowledge, that ye might be filled with all the fullness of God".** All the furnishings you will ever need or could rightly desire are available at the "State Of The Heart" shopping center found only in God's word.

NOTES

NOTES

IX.   GOD IS

[Hebrews 11:6], "But without faith it is impossible to please God: for he that cometh to God must believe that God is, and **that God is a rewarder of them that *diligently* seek him".** God is not presented to us as a theory that needs to be proved by some entity lesser than God himself; an entity that is in possession of a feeble, finite mind that has to learn such simple things as how to tie their shoes, feed and clothe themselves, etc. God presents himself and his creation to his creation as fact based on his own Word of Truth, **[John 17:17], [Romans 3:3-4]. [John 1:1-5], "In the beginning was the Word, and the Word was with God, and the word was God. The same was in the beginning with God. All things were made by him; and without him was not anything made that was made. In him was life; and the life was the light of men. And the light shineth in darkness; and the darkness comprehended it not".**

This darkness is still the problem, as the darkness cannot comprehend it, for the darkness, the world, has no comprehension of the spiritual things of light and life that are given of God and are in Christ. **[Romans 1:18-24]; verse 20, "For the invisible things of him; God, from the creation of the world are clearly seen, being understood by the things that are made, even his eternal Godhead; so that they are without excuse". Verse 22, "Professing themselves to be wise; they became fools".**

Having lived in this world nearly seventy-seven years and observing some of the changes that have come about, I never ceased to be amazed at the abilities that God created in man to accomplish the things that he has been able to accomplish, and yet God gets no credit for such an amazing accomplishment: but it is given to Darwin and his theory of chance evolution. An idiotic world gives Darwin all the credit for the marvelous things God has done and blames God whenever the Darwinists mess things up. It makes me wonder, how can they blame a God they claim doesn't exist?

Considering the fact that man was created in the image and likeness of God with Godlike abilities to be developed and used, but from the beginning, and every since, was and is rejected by man it really isn't very surprising. Man has invented many wonderful and beneficial things, some doubtful and questionable, and some downright destructive and horrendous. Neither is this surprising, given the fact that in [**Genesis 6: 5**], **"And God saw that the wickedness of man was great in the earth and that every imagination of the thoughts of his heart was only evil continually"**. And so it goes with even some of the good things being misused for the promotion of evil purposes.

There are many variations and applications to be made here so we must proceed with caution and wisdom in making applications in these areas. After all, what God created and intended for good, man, has more often than not turned to evil, and some of them exceedingly wretched, but that's not God's doing. Man being created as a "free" moral agent, but in his rebellion, has taken on more of likeness of a bound, immoral agent, bound in slavery to sin because of his chosen, [**Deuteronomy 30: 19**], immorality of death and cursing. Our nation is reeling under multiplied stress and problems because of this pollution of immorality throughout the entire population, even taking its toll in our church world. [**Ephesians 2: 1-3**], **But God, verses 4-10,** this majestic, loving, intervening God, has made a way of deliverance from ourselves and our profound stupidity of sin and iniquity.

The apostle Paul in [**Philippians 1: 7**] makes mention of **"the defense and confirmation of the gospel"**. I can not help but think that if our Christian culture would take on a new and more powerful effect of "boldness and courage", we would put forth more diligent, effective, effort in its conformation and not be so concerned in its defense as the truth has a way of rising to the surface and proving itself regardless of mans attempts to suppress it. **"Truth crushed to the earth shall rise again, the eternal years of God are hers, but error, wounded, writhes in pain and dies among his worshippers".** To live it as the absolute fact that it is, as God has declared it to be, truth, light, and life, with obedience and devotion to God and his will, instead of with questionable erroneous practices and teachings, would allow it to defend itself without argument, dialogue, or debate.

God: who is this God of creation as depicted in his word, this God of the Bible, the God of Israel, of Abraham, Isaac, and Jacob; Jehovah is his name? As we study him, he becomes more interesting and intriguing. Considering that man was originally created in his "image and likeness", with the condition of Godly excellence designed within him, he becomes even more so. It would seem that if man would find out about himself, not what he has reduced himself to, but what God intended him to be; an in depth study of God would be the logical place to start. What I read and study about God, the more he appeals to me as a personage and entity to be emulated. What I have experienced in myself apart from God's influence, conditioning, and re-creation has not been very impressive, some of it downright disgusting and at the very least, quite embarrassing at times. It makes me extremely grateful for God's provision of deliverance through the cleansing power of the blood of Jesus Christ for the remission and forgiveness of sin. There was plenty that needed forgiving. It was not a difficult thing to receive God's forgiveness through **"repentance of sin and believing the gospel"; [Mark 1:15],** the big problem has been in forgiving myself.

The more, however, the enemy and adversary of man's souls has plagued me about my past, the more disgusted with him I have become and the more determined I have become to wage an effective campaign of spiritual warfare against him. I have come to appreciate and value as a pearl of great price, this peace, freedom, and the "blessed assurance" that extends beyond mere hope, of being cleansed by the power of the blood of Jesus, my Lord and Saviour. As the love for God grows and develops within me, the more detestable this Satan, the **"accuser of the brethren" [Revelation 12: 10]** enemy becomes as the Holy Spirit brings to my mind things about this deceiving tempter, some interesting and revealing truths, but he is a subject for another time. He does need to be studied in order to familiarize yourself with his methods, ways, and devices, **[2 Corinthians 2: 11], "lest he get an advantage of you".** It is a wise thing to know your enemy well. It is an extremely wise thing to know God better, for it is his goodness that leads man to repentance and gives us knowledge of what God intended for us to be in his likeness with his excellency designed within us.

Many acknowledge God's existence, and because of their shallow acknowledgement of him, claim to believe in him, knowing nothing about his goodness that he has manifested through Jesus our Lord and Saviour for our redemption and reconciliation back into intimacy of relationship with himself. There is an interesting thought here in conjunction of an earthly marriage of a man and a woman joined together as one flesh, **[Matthew 19: 6]-[Mark 4:9],"What therefore God hath joined together, let not man put asunder".** As God joins man and woman together in intimacy of love and intended spiritual relationship; so he joins us together in an intimacy of the Holy Spirit relationship with himself through Jesus. It can now well be said that what God hath joined together, let not man or devils put asunder. **[John 17],** this Lord's prayer is a clear revelation and application of this desire of the Lord's heart, that we may be one with him; as it is his desire, so should it be ours. It is an unfortunate thing that so many couples do not set themselves to walk together in the Spirit for the sake of a successful marriage, but remain in the flesh without a joining together in the Spirit of the Lord for guidance by the Holy Spirit and direction according to His Word. It is because of this that we are experiencing such an abundance of divorces along with other related problems in the church by many who have professed to being Christians.

Let's examine this Jehovah, God of creation, almighty and all powerful, looking into his character to see what we can find to embrace and enrich our own personalities and character with, for his pleasure and our own well being, as well as those who are within our sphere of influence. Whether you like it or not you are going to influence others and become a contributing factor in their lives. You will, to a certain degree, become a leader in your own right. We won't get it all, we won't live long enough, but we can pretty well keep ourselves busy with **[Hebrews 6:1]**. Too many people get the idea that they can never be perfect, so put forth no effort to **"go on to perfection"**, learning and **[John 8: 29] "doing always those "things" that please the Father"**. Neither do they give diligent heed to the **[Hebrews 6: 9] "better "things" that accompany salvation"** that are essential to the victorious Christian life. These "things", in previously mentioned verses you will find interchangeable, but are by no means a complete list of "things" characteristic of God's divine nature which we are to be partakers of.

Though a person may compile a list of things that give characteristics of God and his nature, it is doubtful we could ever come up with a complete description of all that would do justice to his fullness. We can, however, come up with enough to keep us busy for a lifetime of learning and application. **[Matthew 6:33], "Seek ye first the kingdom of God and his**

righteousness and all these things will be added unto you". Making a study of this scripture alone and attempting to fulfill it is enough to keep anyone busy for their lifetime. "Righteousness" is a rather all inclusive term that contains a multitude of individual items that we need to explore one at a time for clarity and stability. Let's try "patience" as an attribute of God's righteousness; how well are you doing with that one? Do you have it perfected or do you need to do some work on it yet? **[Romans 5: 3],** Have you advanced to a point in your spiritual maturity where you glory in your tribulations, knowing that your tribulations will work patience in your life? **[Hebrews 12; 14] "Follow peace with all men, and holiness, without which no man shall see the Lord".** How are you doing on this holiness thing, and peace; that one sneaked in there with holiness. Are you experiencing great **[Psalms 119: 165],** and perfect **[Isaiah 26:3],** peace on a consistent basis? There are conditions to enjoying these things to this extent. Now we have this Godly characteristic of peace to contend with along with holiness. Either one by itself is a handful, but both at once, what a glorious challenge.

[Psalms 119:165] "Great peace have they that love thy law [word] and nothing shall offend them, or be a stumbling block to them". Great peace; sounds like something of immense value, but now I am faced with the concept of getting an understanding about "love" along with it. We are not used to this much in depth thinking and thought about spiritual concepts all at one time. Our minds are not tuned to nor accustomed to this area of life. We are more used to settling for an existence in this world without all this spiritual stuff including truth too. This is going to involve a changing of our minds. Oh' you call it a renewing of the mind. That's quite and idea; I guess that would be better than just trying to change it. Renewing: would that be like putting a bunch of new stuff of value in my mind to crowd the old worthless, worldly orientated destructive junk out. Not a bad idea huh', and you say I'll find all the new stuff I need to do this in the Bible?

As a matter of fact, that's the only place you will find it. I'll have to admit your right about that, I never did find any of that righteousness, peace, and holiness, nor any of that **[Galatians 5:22-23] Fruit of the Spirit** out in the world. And "forgiveness", there's a good one. All I ever saw in the world was holding grudges, animosity, anger, and revenge, etc, which fed on itself and reproduced itself; usually in a more aggressive form; forgiveness was unheard of. Consequently people were not only angry at every one else **but even at war within themselves, [James 4: 1].** I guess that because God is love, if I want to be like him I need to learn to love like he loves. That is really going to take a major overhauling and renewing of the mind with lots of study and seeking God for direction and guidance as I learn to **"think on the things that please him", [Philippians 4: 6-9],** and enjoy the presence of this "God of peace".

The presence of this God of peace is not only desirable, but an absolute necessity for any successful relationship or ventures you will experience in the course of daily living. Man would do well to put the pursuit and establishing of this intimate relationship with this "God of peace" as the highest and earliest priority of his life, if he wishes and has any hope of experiencing life at its best. Without this there is no life, only a motley existence in what has become a very decrepit world, of man's own making. This creative God of peace never intended it to be this way. Man had his own ideas of how things should be done, and here we are making very feeble attempts to solve the problems we have created by our disobedience and rebellion with the same flawed intelligence that was used to create them. It is getting more difficult each day to acquaint intelligence and the "likeness" of God with humanity. Thank God there are at least a few **[Matthew 7: 14]** exceptions. Man has accomplished many great things in this world by the abilities that God created in him, even to the point, it seems at times, of being a lesser creator himself; however, there does seem to be a considerable amount of discrepancies that have popped up along the way.

Wisdom is an essential element of God's character. We must understand the difference between Godly wisdom and the wisdom of this world. **[James 3: 13-18], "Who is a wise man and endued with knowledge among you? Let him show out of a good conversation his work with meekness of wisdom. But if ye have bitter envying and strife in your hearts, glory not, and lie not against the truth. This wisdom descendeth not from above, but is earthly, sensual, devilish. For where envying and strife is, there is confusion and every evil work. But the wisdom that is from above is first pure, then peaceable, gentle, and easy to be entreated, full of mercy and good fruits, without partiality, and without hypocrisy. And the fruit of righteousness is sown in peace of them that make peace".** This section of scripture gives us vital information relating to the difference between the wisdom of God and the wisdom of this world and the individuals that are characterized by each one. **[Matthew 7: 19-20], verse 20 "Wherefore by their fruits ye shall know them".** A man's own fruit will judge him. **[Matthew 3: 8], "Bring forth therefore fruits meet for repentance".**

There are other elements of Godliness mentioned along with wisdom here, so lets take a closer look as each one of these things, each in itself fill an entire area of need that we all have in our individual lives. **[Psalms 111:10], "The fear, reverencing, of the Lord is the beginning of wisdom: a good understanding have all they that do his commandments".** **[Proverbs 1:7], "The fear of the Lord is the beginning of knowledge: but fools despise wisdom and instruction".** **[Proverbs 9:10], "The fear of the Lord is the beginning of wisdom: and the knowledge of the holy is understanding".**

[Proverbs 4:7] "Wisdom is the principle thing; therefore get wisdom: and with all thy getting get understanding". We have touched on wisdom, understanding, and knowledge and each one need personal attention as to study and application. These things, as others, are easier to study than to apply. There is one other that is not mentioned in the Bible which may well allude to all the others combined and yet be contained within them, that is Godly "intelligence" that prompts and proceeds from the mind renewed in Christ, conforming to the Word of God. The getting of "wisdom that is from above" is one thing; however, the keeping, maintaining, and developing of it to the enrichment of humanity has seemed to be quite beyond us and requires a considerable amount of attention, practice; and patience. Intelligence, operative within the renewed mind, in its truest sense would well demand this while the earthly, sensual, and as yet un-renewed, corrupted mind of man can not even comprehend such an intelligence and its requirements of righteousness, holiness, and Biblical absolutes. There are a whole host of things to be considered in our **[Romans 8:1] "walking in the spirit and not after the flesh"** in relationship with God.

We have touched on but a few things here that include others which must be sought out for the specifics involved. The term "things" is rather an inclusive term in which are many specifics that make up the "things" referred to. For instance in **[Hebrews 6: 9] the better "things" that accompany salvation** are not named, but are nevertheless referred to for study and accomplishment and are to be found throughout the scriptures. Some of these "things" include, but are not limited to, the list in **[Galatians 5: 22-23] naming the Fruit of the Spirit.** These "things" among other "things" are very descriptive of the character which God originally intended for us to have as those that were made in his image and likeness and give us valuable insight into the heart and divine nature of God.

134

[2 Peter 1: 2-11] "Grace and peace be multiplied unto you through the knowledge of God, and of Jesus our Lord, According as his divine power hath given unto us all things that pertain unto life and godliness, through the knowledge of him that hath called us to glory and virtue: Whereby are given unto us exceeding great and precious promises: that by these ye might be partakers of the divine nature, having escaped the corruption that is in the world through lust. And besides this, giving all diligence, add to your faith virtue; and to virtue knowledge; And to knowledge temperance; and to temperance patience; and to patience godliness; And to godliness brotherly kindness; and to brotherly kindness, [1 Corinthians 13] charity. For if these things be in you, and abound, they make you that ye shall neither be barren nor unfruitful in the knowledge of our Lord Jesus Christ. BUT he that lacketh these things is blind, and cannot see afar off, and hath forgotten that he was purged from his old sins. Wherefore the rather, brethren, give diligence to make your calling and election sure: FOR IF YE DO THESE "THINGS", YE SHALL NEVER FALL: for so an entrance shall be ministered unto you abundantly into the everlasting kingdom of our Lord and Saviour Jesus Christ". In verses 12-15 of this 1st chapter of Peter, he emphasizes the necessity of our **"always being in remembrance of these things"**. These are **"things that accompany salvation"**, some of which are not on the list of the Fruit of the Spirit, but nevertheless must be included with them, for they do indeed proceed from the Holy Spirit. This is part of the promise, and in conjunction with **[John 14:26], "But the Comforter, which is the Holy Ghost, whom the Father will send in my name, he shall teach you all "things", and bring all "things" to your remembrance, whatsoever I have said unto you".**

Let's face it, we, humanity, need all the help we can get to be delivered from our dungeons and prisons of stupidity, ignorance, and idiocy. The conditions of our lives, families, churches, states, nations, indeed the whole world are all vivid testimonies to the fact that we have been in these dungeons and prisons much to long without the depth of belief in God and the diligence needed in seeking him in order to receive the rewards he has promised those who **"diligently seek him"** for intimacy of relationship. As to what the extent of these "rewards" are; lets just say they are all included in Jesus and the **"life and life more abundantly"** he came to give to those who will **"repent and believe the gospel" unto obedience, [John 10:10]-[Mark 1: 15].** These rewards are not listed so far as a list is concerned, but are to be found throughout God's word as precious treasure is to be sought and worthy of the effort involved and energy expended in the discovery of each and every one. The problem is that so many people do not attach value to these things so don't even know what they have when they find it. Having these treasures is one thing, recognizing them for what they are is another and the source of provision, and all this is useless without the knowledge and desire to skillfully and diligently use them for their intended purpose. For instance, you may have a dozen Bibles around your house, on shelves, in desk drawers or wherever, that are collecting dust, occasionally picked up and "thumbed through, but seldom read or ever actually studied for the purpose of application.

One well used, applied Bible will prove more valuable to a person than a stack of them unused; though they in themselves, because of their content, are extremely valuable. They are intended to be used, **God intends for his [John 15: 3] written and spoken word to be applied for effect; and it can only have effect if it is applied: [Romans 2: 13], "For not the hearers of the law [word] are just before God, but the doers of the law [word] shall be justified".** With this in mind the, **[John 15: 3] becomes "Now ye are clean through the *"applied"* word which I have spoken unto you".** This is further emphasized in a scripture that has become quite familiar to the serious Christian element within the church, [2 Timothy 2:15], "Study to show thyself approved unto God, a workman that needeth not to be ashamed, rightly dividing the word of truth". [1 Peter 1:15-16] "But as he which hath called you is holy, so be ye holy in all manner of conversation; because it is written, be ye holy; for I am holy". [Hebrews 12: 14], "Follow peace with all men, and holiness, *without which no man shall see the Lord*".

NOTES

NOTES

NOTES

NOTES